W W J D

Interactive Devotional

dc talk

Top

the newsboys

CCM Artists

audio adrenaline

Answer

big tent revival

One Tough

steven curtis chapman

Question

rebecca st. james

and others

Compiled by
Dana Key

WWJD Interactive Devotional
Copyright © 1997 by The Zondervan Corporation
Requests for information should be addressed to:
ZondervanPublishingHouse
Grand Rapids, Michigan 49530

ISBN: 0-310-22234-6

Interior design by PAZ Design Group

Printed in the United States of America

98 99 00 01 02 03 04 /❖ DC/ 10 9 8

Contents

The Challenge

Choices. Our lives are filled with them. Each day we make dozens of choices. Some are big: Whom will I date? Where will I go to college? Whom should I hang out with? But let's face it, most of our choices aren't going to rock the world no matter which way we decide. This book is not about whether you should wear the green shirt or the black one (black is always safe). Who cares if you have the pepperoni pizza or the mixed vegetables? (Besides your mother.)

This book is about the moral choices you make each day. Whether you know it or not, each of them will affect the outcome of your life—and your eternal destiny.

Peter tells us that "Christ suffered for you, leaving you an example, that you should follow in his steps" (1 Peter 2:21). The concept here is that we don't have to draw straws or flip a coin every time we choose. For many of the "toughies" that we face, we can simply look back and ask, "What did Jesus do in this situation?" Peter says that Jesus is "our example." Thus, if we can figure out how Jesus acted or reacted in a similar situation, we can do what he did and rest assured we've done the right thing.

Now, I'm sure someone is thinking, "Hey, Jesus lived nearly 2000 years ago. How could his experiences be relative to mine? Well, you might be surprised. No, Jesus was never cut off in five o'clock traffic, and no one ever stuck crack cocaine in his face, but he did live in a world filled with racism, murder, prostitution, and government corruption. As far as we know, he didn't have a girlfriend, but he did have at least six brothers and sisters. He held a real job, went to parties. He even had a close "so-called friend" who stabbed him in the back. He experienced loneliness, joy, anxiety, and anger. Sometimes he laughed and other times he cried. The only big difference between Jesus and us is: He never sinned. The Bible says that Jesus "has been tempted in every way, just as we are—yet was without sin" (Hebrews 4:15).

A zillion books have been written about what Jesus said, and for good reason, but for the next thirty days, we would like you to do two things. Think about what Jesus did, and every time you have to make a meaningful choice, ask yourself this simple question, "What Would Jesus Do?"

Steve Wiggins

BIG TENT REVIVAL

When I sat down to write a song that asks, "What would Jesus do?" I didn't want it to sound superficial. I didn't want it to say, "You're at a party and someone offers you pot, so what would Jesus do?" The answer is too obvious. Or I'm in the back seat of my car with my girlfriend, "What would Jesus do?" Jesus wouldn't have been in the back seat of the car with his girlfriend in the first place.

The other potential pitfall in a song about what Jesus would do is sounding like you're making the Christian life into a set of rules. I heard Dr. Adrian Rogers say, "Children live by rules and adults live by principles." Our

Some people just want to survive
And I don't know about you, but I am alive
Lately it seems that I need a hand in
*   a fallen world*
I just want to stand. And as we all know,
*   life can be tough*
And all that we need is love—sweet love
So where do we go? Well, here's what I see
To change my world, I gotta change me
What would Jesus do walkin' in my shoes
Workin' at my job and goin' to my school
And I hear people say, "Jesus is the way"
I believe and that is why I'm asking you
What would Jesus do?
Sometimes choices don't seem black and white
And they can leave you black and blue
What would Jesus do—He'd give his life for you
If you follow Him—you'll give your life to them
Shine on—shine on—follow with Jesus.

"What Would Jesus Do?"
Big Tent Revival

human tendency is to look for a rule rather than a principle because it simplifies the decision-making process. The problem is that real choices are seldom that black and white. We want a clear system of right and wrong, but most choices don't fit into those compartments that neatly.

I think that was what caused the Pharisees in Jesus' day to make up a mountain of rules to live under. They took the simple laws that God had given and subdivided them, adding to them and changing them to the point that they became a burden too big for anyone to bear.

Then Jesus came along and said, "If you want to know what the Law of God is, I can sum it up in these two simple principles: 'Love the LORD your God with all your heart, soul and mind and … love your neighbor as yourself.'" I mean, that's it! When you make a choice you have to consider, "Does this help me to love God more?" and "How does this choice affect my neighbor?" That's a little more complex than just following a list of do's and don'ts.

The good news is that, in the Bible, we have a complete record of not only what Jesus said, but also how he applied these two principles himself. As you turn every page you see that his life was a perfect example. He loved his Father completely and he gave his own life for you and me.

What Would Jesus Do?

He grew up before him like a tender shoot, and like a root out of dry ground. He had no beauty or majesty to attract us to him, nothing in his appearance that we should desire him. He was despised and rejected by men, a man of sorrows, and familiar with suffering. Like one from whom men hide their faces he was despised, and we esteemed him not.

Surely he took up our infirmities and carried our sorrows, yet we considered him stricken by God, smitten by him, and afflicted. But he was pierced for our transgressions, he was crushed for our iniquities; the punishment that brought us peace was upon him, and by his wounds we are healed. We all, like sheep, have gone astray, each of us has turned to his own way; and the LORD has laid on him the iniquity of us all.

He was oppressed and afflicted, yet he did not open his mouth; he was led like a lamb to the slaughter, and as a sheep before her shearers is silent, so he did not open his mouth. By oppression and judgment he was taken away. And who can speak of his descendants? For he was cut off from the land of the living; for the transgression of my people he was stricken. He was assigned a grave with the wicked, and with the rich in his death, though he had done no violence, nor was any deceit in his mouth.

Yet it was the LORD's will to crush him and cause him to suffer, and though the LORD makes his life a guilt offering, he will see his offspring and prolong his days, and the will of the LORD will prosper in his hand. After the suffering of his soul, he will see the light [of life] and be satisfied; by his knowledge my righteous servant will justify many, and he will bear their iniquities. Therefore I will give him a portion among the great, and he will divide the spoils with the strong, because he poured out his life unto death, and was numbered with the transgressors. For he bore the sin of many, and made intercession for the transgressors. (Isaiah 53:2–12)

 # The Point!

The Christian life is not about keeping a set of rules, it's about doing all you can to love God and give yourself to others. You might think, "That's great, no rules!" Not so fast. It may work just the opposite from what you're thinking.

If you made a list of every rule you could possibly think of, eventually you would run into some moral choices that hadn't been covered in the so-called "complete set of rules." In that event you could do what ever you wished. But on the other hand, if you ditch the rule book and make every decision with loving God and serving your neighbor as your guide, you'll have a road map for all of life's choices.

What Should You Do?

If you were on your way to church but ran across a motorist who needed help, what would you do?

> I really don't know.
>
> I'd probably just keep going, thinking "It's someone else's problem, They'll help him"

When Jesus tells us to love our "neighbors" as ourselves, who do you think he means?

> Everyone

What are some of the things you could do to increase your love for God?

> Take time out of every day to just spend time w/ him.

Mark Stuart

AUDIO ADRENALINE

I've felt for a long time that the church needs to be better in tune with the basic everyday needs of people. And when I say "the church," I mean me, you, and everyone who claims to know Jesus. Churches have the tendency to spend a lot of time talking about sermons, doctrine, and theological issues, while there are real people hurting out there on the streets.

Don't get me wrong, theology is important, but it shouldn't take so much of our time that we have no time left to help a family that needs food or a fourteen-year-old girl who's just discovered she's pregnant. If we never get around to dealing with these kind of problems, in my view, we are just playing at being the church.

When you see Jesus in the Bible, he's not just interested in a person's soul. He's dealing with the

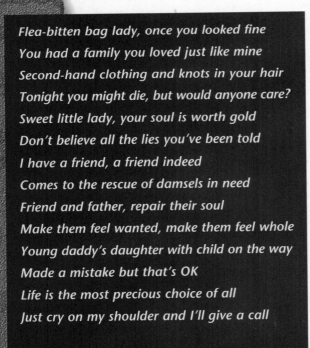

Flea-bitten bag lady, once you looked fine
You had a family you loved just like mine
Second-hand clothing and knots in your hair
Tonight you might die, but would anyone care?
Sweet little lady, your soul is worth gold
Don't believe all the lies you've been told
I have a friend, a friend indeed
Comes to the rescue of damsels in need
Friend and father, repair their soul
Make them feel wanted, make them feel whole
Young daddy's daughter with child on the way
Made a mistake but that's OK
Life is the most precious choice of all
Just cry on my shoulder and I'll give a call

"Bag Lady"
Audio Adrenaline

whole person. He doesn't force the five thousand to hear his sermon over the growling of their empty stomachs. He feeds them. He doesn't just tell the lame man, "Your sins are forgiven and good luck with your disability." He tells him to "rise up and walk" and then he empowers him to do it.

If we're ever going to really reach our world for Christ, we're going to have to start with the wounded, the abandoned, and the helpless people that we pass in our cars every day. If we would shift our priorities to them, the church would experience incredible revival.

What Would Jesus Do?

Some time later, Jesus went up to Jerusalem for a feast of the Jews. Now there is in Jerusalem near the Sheep Gate a pool, which in Aramaic is called Bethesda and which is surrounded by five covered colonnades. Here a great number of disabled people used to lie—the blind, the lame, the paralyzed. One who was there had been an invalid for thirty-eight years. When Jesus saw him lying there and learned that he had been in this condition for a long time, he asked him, "Do you want to get well?"

"Sir," the invalid replied, "I have no one to help me into the pool when the water is stirred. While I am trying to get in, someone else goes down ahead of me."

Then Jesus said to him, "Get up! Pick up your mat and walk." At once the man was cured; he picked up his mat and walked.

The day on which this took place was a Sabbath, and so the Jews said to the man who had been healed, "It is the Sabbath; the law forbids you to carry your mat." But he replied, "The man who made me well said to me, "Pick up your mat and walk."

So they asked him, "Who is this fellow who told you to pick it up and walk?"

The man who was healed had no idea who it was, for Jesus had slipped away into the crowd that was there. (John 5:1–13)

The Point!

The Pharisees were an amazingly devout group of religious people. They studied the Laws of the Old Testament more carefully than any group on earth, yet missed the point of why the Jewish Laws were given in the first place.

When Jesus healed the crippled man at the pool of Bethesda, you would think the Pharisees would have shouted, "Praise God, take us to the man who performed this miracle." Sure, they wanted to find Jesus, but it wasn't to thank him for this man's healing. It was to punish him. Performing miracles on the Sabbath was out of bounds, and so was telling the lame man to pick up his mat and walk.

No one knew the Bible better than the Pharisees. No group spent more time discussing and debating Scripture. Yet through the years their priorities got turned upside down. Keeping the rules and protecting tradition were more important to them than seeing a neighbor made whole. For all their hours of public prayers and religious debates, it never occurred to the Pharisees that God might care more about meeting the needs of wounded people than fruitless hours of empty talk. After all, the Law the Pharisees professed to love so dearly was not given to keep people in bondage, it was given to keep them from being injured in the first place.

If we expect a wounded world to recognize that God's heart beats within his people, they'll need to see the two things that Jesus demonstrated daily. First, God is concerned with the whole person (body and soul). And second, talk minus action equals zero.

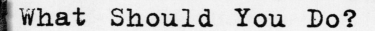

What Should You Do?

Who are the wounded in your community? Does your community have any problems with homelessness, teenage pregnancy, or drugs and alcohol?

Have you ever visited a rescue mission or a soup kitchen? If you haven't, why not?

What kind of project could you and your friends cook up to help someone who needs you?

Rebecca St.James

"Go And Sin No More" was of course inspired by that wonderful story in the gospel of John where a woman was caught in adultery and brought before Jesus. This is one of those passages of Scripture I love so dearly because you can really see into the heart of Jesus. First, Jesus disbanded the woman's self-righteous accusers by inviting the sinless among them to cast the first stones. And then he tenderly forgave her, saying, "Go and sin no more." This is a story about the kind of hope that comes from forgiveness.

My generation is desperately seeking a place to find hope. Young people are being forced to grow up far earlier these days than in the past. The media, our culture, and Hollywood are exposing kids to the kind of choices they are not prepared for. And many are making very bad choices. At an incredibly young age many of my gen-

---

I've sinned come on my knees—
for I'm not worthy of your love
How could you die for me—
such grace could only come from God
Oh Lord, you search and you know me—
you see me inside out
God, you alone can forgive me—
erase my fear and my doubt
Father you pick me up—
I feel like a child in your arms
I don't deserve this love but, I hear
your voice Lord Jesus
Go and sin no more
He said, "I will not condemn you, I'll
forgive and I'll forget it all"
Go and sin no more
"My child let me remind you it is I
who'll lead and guide you as you go"

"Go And Sin No More"
Rebecca St. James

eration already have a long list of regrets and experiences they would like to forget. I think it's this kind of hurt that accounts for much of the hopelessness I see. And it's the same kind of worthless feeling that the woman in this story might have been feeling (until Jesus restored her hope).

Two nights ago, I met a young man at my Nashville concert who confirmed to me how powerful hope and forgiveness can be. He told me that his fiancé left him, and because of that, he had been contemplating suicide. By an act of God, my song came on the radio at just the right time earlier that afternoon and really touched him. When he heard it, he broke down in tears and right there made up his mind that he was going to live!

It was so cool to be standing there looking this man in the eyes, knowing that "Go And Sin No More" had a part in saving his life. I felt so incredibly humbled that God would redeem a life like that using my simple song. I was in awe of God and amazed by the way he is still working miracles all around us. The very same words spoken by Jesus that restored that woman's life nearly two thousand years ago gave that young man back his life last week. It just shows you the majesty of God and the power of hope.

What Would Jesus Do?

The teachers of the law and the Pharisees brought in a woman caught in adultery. They made her stand before the group and said to Jesus, "Teacher, this woman was caught in the act of adultery. In the Law Moses commanded us to stone such women. Now what do you say?" They were using this question as a trap, in order to have a basis for accusing him.

But Jesus bent down and started to write on the ground with his finger. When they kept on questioning him, he straightened up and said to them, "If any one of you is without sin, let him be the first to throw a stone at her." Again he stooped down and wrote on the ground.

At this, those who heard began to go away one at a time, the older ones first, until only Jesus was left, with the woman still standing there.

Jesus straightened up and asked her, "Woman, where are they? Has no one condemned you?"

"No one, sir," she said.

"Then neither do I condemn you," Jesus declared. "Go now and leave your life of sin." (John 8:3–11)

The Point!

One of the consequences of sin the Serpent never prepared Adam and Eve for was guilt. For the first time ever, they felt estranged from God. His calls to them in the garden had once seemed inviting, even comforting. The fellowship during their evening walks was wonderful. But now their disobedience left them feeling dirty and ashamed. Now they were afraid of God, so they hid.

Guilt is a poison that can destroy your self-worth and drive you further from sin's only cure. The apostle Paul warns that there is worldly sorrow that leads to death. Some might say it more than leads you there, it shoves you. Worldly sorrow continually shouts in your ear, "You are worthless to God and when he gets his hands on you, it's going to be awful!"

The devil is dreadfully aware of the power of worldly sorrow. He uses it against us with such incredible skill and stealth that sometimes it can be days or years before we realize we have been running away from the One who truly loves us. Satan may even come to us quoting Scripture. The one he often uses on me is John 1:8, "If we say we have no sin we lie and the truth is not in us." But you can bet that the "Accuser of the Brethren" will never slip up and continue on to the very next verse, "If we confess our sin, he is faithful and just to forgive us our sin and cleanse us from all unrighteousness."

What Should You Do?

What is something in your past you need to talk to Jesus about?

Do you feel that God is big enough and kind enough to forgive you? Why or why not?

After God forgives you, will you forgive yourself?

Pete Stewart

GRAMMATRAIN

I grew up in what you might call a hyper-Pentecostal church. I was around an environment where people lived a Christian life that seemed to rest heavily on emotion. That's what I ended up basing my faith on, and it proved to be a pretty fragile foundation. My emotional state became sort of a litmus test of whether or not I was saved. I thought if I felt good that must mean I was doing good. But I had no idea what to do or think when I felt depressed. Did feeling bad mean I wasn't not saved and God had some how left me for some reason? It was a very schizophrenic way to live. One day I felt filled with belief, and another I doubted I really knew what it was to be a Christian.

Even though I grew up in a great Christian home, it wasn't until I moved out that I started coming to grips with all this. When I found myself out on my own I started really thinking for myself and questioning exactly what I believed. I no longer wanted to rely on my parents' beliefs; I had to find out on my own.

Maybe the most important thing that happened during this time was that I enrolled in Bible college. It may seem like a weird place for someone who is questioning his or her faith to be, and it certainly was. Bible college brought a whole

> *Jesus and his disciples went on to the villages around Caesarea Philippi. On the way he asked them, "Who do people say I am?" They replied, "Some say John the Baptist; others say Elijah; and still others, one of the prophets." "But what about you?" he asked. "Who do you say I am?" Peter answered, "You are the Christ."*
>
> *Mark 8:27–29*

new set of rules to Christianity I wasn't aware of: proper length of hair, proper attire, proper worship style, and the proper smile. Needless to say, these "extra regulations" did not satisfy my hunger to discover the truth. Instead, they drove me to challenge my faith all the more.

After a couple of years of soul searching, I found that although my fragile view of what I thought Christianity was had fallen and shattered to pieces, the truth of Scripture and of who Christ said he was stood firm and strong. I had learned something much more important than how to feel good; I learned what truth was. Truth doesn't change with the weather; truth is truth whether I feel lousy or "pumped and excited." God knows I'm a very fallible human being and his existence is not threatened by that.

Through all the questioning my faith became one hundred times stronger. The whole experience taught me that it's all right to question your faith because Christianity can stand up to any close examination. What value would your faith have if you lived in fear that close scrutiny would poke holes in it?

Since I've discovered that Christianity can stand up to any test, I also believe sincere questioning will lead people to faith and not away from it. I'm convinced that anyone who questions the claims of Christ with intellectual honesty will come to the same conclusion that I did: He is the ultimate truth.

What Would Jesus Do?

"I told you that you would die in your sins; if you do not believe that I am [the one I claim to be], you will indeed die in your sins."

"Who are you?" they asked.

"Just what I have been claiming all along," Jesus replied....

"I tell you the truth, if anyone keeps my word, he will never see death."

At this the Jews exclaimed, "Now we know that you are demon-possessed!

Abraham died and so did the prophets, yet you say that if anyone keeps your word, he will never taste death. Are you greater than our father Abraham? He died, and so did the prophets. Who do you think you are?"

Jesus replied, "If I glorify myself, my glory means nothing. My Father, whom you claim as your God, is the one who glorifies me. Though you do not know him, I know him. If I said I did not, I would be a liar like you, but I do know him and keep his word. Your father Abraham rejoiced at the thought of seeing my day; he saw it and was glad."

"You are not yet fifty years old," the Jews said to him, "and you have seen Abraham!"

"I tell you the truth," Jesus answered, "before Abraham was born, I am!" At this, they picked up stones to stone him, but Jesus hid himself, slipping away from the temple grounds. (John 8:24–25, 51–59)

The Point!

C. S. Lewis brilliantly observed that in sizing up Jesus Christ you only have three options. He is either a brilliant liar, a raging lunatic, or the Lord of all. Now, if he is a liar, he is both an amazing liar and a fool at the same time. Amazing in that he not only fooled his closest friends into believing but also his own family. I don't know about you, but I can never sneak anything past my mom. Can you imagine trying to pass yourself off as God to your own family? And yet if he indeed was a liar, he was a fool, because he died for a lie that he could have easily retracted. He didn't get rich. His lie brought him nothing but pain.

The second option is that he was insane. But could a nut

case confound the scholarship of the Sadducees and Pharisees? Would he be able to amaze them at the tender age of twelve? Could he have preached the Sermon on the Mount or formulated such amazing parables? And if he were a lunatic, would God have given him the power to walk on water and raise the dead? You might say, "I never saw him do any of that stuff." The disciples who walked with him for three and a half years surely did, and they were convinced enough to die for their beliefs.

So that leaves us with one final choice. If he wasn't a liar and couldn't have been a lunatic, then he must have been who he claimed to be: Lord.

What Should You Do?

What kinds of questions do you have about your faith?

In what ways have you taken the time to really investigate the things you believe to see if they are so?

Would you die for your faith in Jesus? Will you live for Him?

Michael Johnston

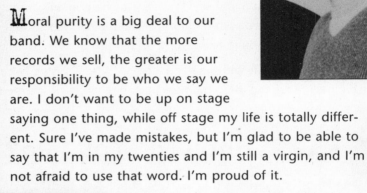

Moral purity is a big deal to our band. We know that the more records we sell, the greater is our responsibility to be who we say we are. I don't want to be up on stage saying one thing, while off stage my life is totally different. Sure I've made mistakes, but I'm glad to be able to say that I'm in my twenties and I'm still a virgin, and I'm not afraid to use that word. I'm proud of it.

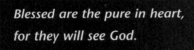

Blessed are the pure in heart, for they will see God.

Matthew 5:8

I'm not going to tell you that being morally pure is not a constant battle. It's very, very difficult. But I've found there are certain things we can do as Christians that really help. First of all, there are some situations you just stay away from. For instance, our band has a rule that we don't bring girls onto our tour bus. That's a recipe for disaster. So we just stay away from it completely.

Another rule we've made, thanks to Mike, our road manager, is we're careful about the movies we watch on the bus. We self-censor sex scenes and rough language. Look, I'm a normal guy. If I'm going to keep my moral compass pointed in the right direction, I just have to pass on a lot of those movies that some people call "harmless entertainment."

Finally, I read a lot. It's not enough to keep the bad stuff out of your mind; you've got to put the right stuff in. Though I'm not a big fiction fan, I do love the writings of

C. S. Lewis. And, of course, I spend a lot of time reading my Bible. God's Word is a real source of moral strength. Out on the road, there are plenty of long travel hours. I'm learning to make good use of them.

What Did Joseph Do?

So he left in Joseph's care everything he had; with Joseph in charge, he did not concern himself with anything except the food he ate.

Now Joseph was well-built and handsome, and after a while his master's wife took notice of Joseph and said, "Come to bed with me!"

But he refused. "With me in charge," he told her, "my master does not concern himself with anything in the house; everything he owns he has entrusted to my care. No one is greater in this house than I am. My master has withheld nothing from me except you, because you are his wife. How then could I do such a wicked thing and sin against God?" And though she spoke to Joseph day after day, he refused to go to bed with her or even be with her.

One day he went into the house to attend to his duties, and none of the household servants was inside. She caught him by his cloak and said, "Come to bed with me!" But he left his cloak in her hand and ran out of the house. (Genesis 39:6–12)

The Point!

Today we live in the midst of the so-called "sexual revolution." Virginity is ridiculed and abstinence is called unrealistic. Teachers give out condoms, senators participate in gay and lesbian pride parades, and entertainers sing about sex acts in such vivid language that no imagination is required. Like a giant pipeline, videos, D-TV, satellite dishes, cable, and the Internet pump one consistent message into our homes: "In an enlightened society sex outside of marriage is normal."

As a result, since 1973, our "enlightened society" has seen twenty-five million abortions. Reported rapes have more than doubled. Teenage pregnancy is out of control. Sexually transmitted diseases such as syphilis and gonorrhea have dramatically increased. And a new killer called AIDS is infecting millions worldwide.

Is God against sex? Of course not; he created it. But his ideal for sex is that it would serve as a special and holy way to unite one man and one women for life. Sex enjoyed in this way is a special gift from God that is worth waiting for.

What Should You Do?

Are you willing to say no to sex before marriage, even if it means losing someone you think is very special? What kind of support would you need to stick by your decision?

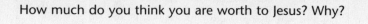

How much do you think you are worth to Jesus? Why?

What would you say to someone who felt that their immorality was too grave a sin for God to forgive?

Steven Curtis Chapman

Last night I got a little uptight and I kind of lost it for a moment. I was talking to my wife, Mary Beth, from my hotel room, and I heard this knock on the door. It was the road manager telling me to hurry up and get on the bus. I shouldn't have let it get to me, but I guess I was just frustrated by being constantly on someone else's schedule. I hung up the phone, threw my stuff on the bus, and slammed the door. As hard as I could.

I felt bad. Sure, I could have justified my little tantrum. I was away from my family. I was physically tired. Pitching a little fit once in a while is a very natural way to let off steam. But that's just the point. While it was a very easy and natural thing for me to do, there is no no justification for it in God's sight. God expects much more of me than that.

I remember hearing my pastor preach on the verse where Paul tells the Corinthians to quit acting like "mere men"

Mirror, mirror on the wall
Who's the biggest fool of all
You don't have to answer me
'Cause when I look at you I see
A prisoner set free from his chains
Acting like he's still a slave
To the prison he's been set free from
You may say it's only natural for me
  to act his way
Well I know it's only natural
But I have not been made …
Only natural, only natural
I've got the Spirit of the living God
  alive in me
Giving me power so I don't have to be
Only natural, only natural

"Only Natural"
Steven Curtis Chapman

(1 Corinthians 3:3). His point was that their behavior might be typical out in the world, but it's not the way believers should act. I mean, we have God's Word and his Spirit. We've been made new creations and we're part of the body of Christ. We're told that "by his divine power we have been given everything we need for life and godliness" (2 Peter 1:3). I'm no longer a natural man, I'm supernatural, and God expects me to live life according to the new nature he gives me.

The standards have gotten much higher since I trusted Christ. For a moment last night, I forgot that. Oh, and by the way, I apologized to the guys, and just like always, they forgave me for acting like I was "only human."

What Would Jesus Do?

Then they went to a place called Gethsemane, and Jesus said to his disciples, "Sit here while I pray." He took Peter, James and John along with him, and he began to be deeply distressed and troubled. "My soul is overwhelmed with sorrow to the point of death," he said to them. "Stay here and keep watch."

Going a little farther, he fell to the ground and prayed that if possible the hour might pass from him. "Abba, Father," he said, "everything is possible for you. Take this cup from me. Yet not what I will, but what you will." (Mark 14:32–36)

The Point!

A student told his Sunday school teacher that he didn't believe the book of Genesis. He was convinced that human beings came from monkeys. The teacher reprimanded him, saying, "Son, in my class, I forbid you to talk so disparagingly about defenseless little monkeys. Men couldn't have come from such noble animals. Monkeys don't leave their wives, do drugs, start wars, or live on the street. Furthermore, a monkey would never consider killing its young or letting them starve."

Unlike monkeys, ever since the Garden of Eden, the standard-issue human being comes complete with a morally flawed guidance system. When people "let their hearts be their guides," they get lost morally because their hearts are damaged from birth. Consequently, we don't have to tune in to prime-time TV to see *Men Behaving Badly*. Men (and women) behave badly all around us every day because it's "human nature."

By contrast, Christians have a choice. We've been given a brand new nature. This new nature always leads us into the footsteps of Jesus. Our problem is that the old morally flawed guidance system is still lurking around inside, and it still wants to steer. The question is, which nature will you put in the driver's seat of your life?

 # What Should You Do?

How do you distinguish God's will from your own?

Do you have a temper problem? What really gets to you?

In what ways should your lifestyle look different from that of a non-Christian friend?

Jeff Frankenstein

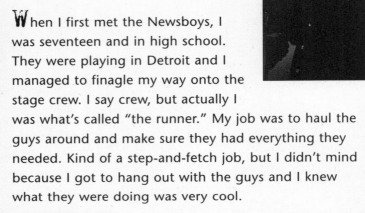

When I first met the Newsboys, I was seventeen and in high school. They were playing in Detroit and I managed to finagle my way onto the stage crew. I say crew, but actually I was what's called "the runner." My job was to haul the guys around and make sure they had everything they needed. Kind of a step-and-fetch job, but I didn't mind because I got to hang out with the guys and I knew what they were doing was very cool.

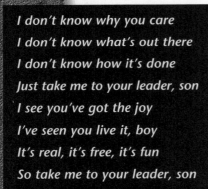

I don't know why you care
I don't know what's out there
I don't know how it's done
Just take me to your leader, son
I see you've got the joy
I've seen you live it, boy
It's real, it's free, it's fun
So take me to your leader, son

"Take Me To Your Leader"
Newsboys

One particular day, I was taking Peter over to the auditorium and mentioned that I was a keyboard player. Little did I know that bit of information would turn my life around. Peter acted interested, but I thought he was just being a nice guy. I assumed he would forget my name the very next day.

Well, two years later I came home from a college class and my mom told me that some guy with a funny accent had called. Lo and behold, it was Peter calling after two whole years! He said the band was looking for a keyboard player. We discovered that the Newsboys were going to be in Michigan the very next week. Peter suggested I drop by the show. And he also suggested I learn some of their new songs.

Man, I went to work! I took off from school for three days and practiced like crazy. When the big day came I was really nervous at the afternoon audition, but I must have done okay, because the band asked me if I would like to stick around and do the concert that night. After the show, the band asked me if I thought I was ready to join up with the Newsboys. I couldn't believe it.

I went home in shock. This was like a fairy tale, and yet it was all moving so fast. I felt totally unprepared. I was only nineteen and I was going to have to leave my family, my friends, and school. It was a hard choice for me. I know most people would say, "Man, are you crazy? It's the Newsboys who want you!" But so far this has been the biggest leap of faith God has ever asked me to make.

I guess you've figured out by now that I went for it. And I have absolutely no regrets. Looking back, I can see how this was all God's timing. Even though it was hard to see at first, God had been preparing me for this mission throughout my life. He knew where I was supposed to go; it was just up to me to say, "Yes, God, I am ready to go where you lead."

What Would Jesus Do?

"Don't you believe that I am in the Father, and that the Father is in me? The words I say to you are not just my own. Rather, it is the Father, living in me, who is doing his work. Believe me when I say that I am in the Father and the Father is in me; or at least believe on the evidence of the miracles themselves. I tell you the truth, anyone who has faith in me will do what I have been doing. He will do even greater things than these, because I am going to the Father. And I will do whatever you ask in my name, so that the Son may bring glory to the Father. You may ask me for anything in my name, and I will do it. If you love me, you will obey what I command." (John 14:10–15)

The Point!

Karl Wallenda was the Babe Ruth of aerialists. Once, as a promotional gimmick, he walked a high wire two hundred feet above Niagara Falls. When onlookers noticed a man walking confidently over the rocks and water, they began to cheer wildly. One wrong step would mean certain death.

Karl walked out to the halfway point and then back. Laying aside his balance beam he took a wheel barrow and pushed it across as the crowd shouted their approval. Karl made his way back to the hysterical crowd and said, "Ladies and gentlemen, do you think I can put a person in this wheel barrow and push it to the other side?"

The crowd went wild with affirmation. Then Karl asked that now famous question, "Who will volunteer?" As the crowd fell silent, one little voice spoke up and said, "I will."

What the audience and press didn't know was that Karl knew no one would volunteer but the little girl. The little girl had been told to volunteer. She was Karl's daughter. She was more than willing to comply. She knew her daddy could safely push her across the high wire. He had done it dozens of times before in other cities.

Karl's daughter obeyed her father and got into the wheel barrow because of three things. One, she was told to. Two, she believed her father was willing to keep her safe. And three, she knew he was able. These are the same compelling things that cause us to obey God.

Some say that faith is blind. And what they mean by that is that faith is not based on good common sense. But that kind of "faith" is not biblical faith, but superstition. Real faith is based on good solid information and therefore makes great sense.

Christians must never leap without answering three questions. These answers form the three links of a chain that can securely keep us above the deepest chasm of doubt. The first is, "Has God asked me to jump?" The second is, "Is God willing to catch me?" And the final link is, "Is he able to do what he has promised?" When we know we've heard his voice, when we trust that he loves us, and when we are confident that he rules the world, leaps of faith are a piece of cake. Though we dangle over the Grand Canyon, we rest in the confidence that we are held firmly by this unbreakable three-link chain of faith.

What Should You Do?

Do you think God is preparing you for a mission of faith? What might it be?

Looking back at either your upbringing or your talents, what kind of glimpses do you get of what God may want you to do in the future?

In what ways are you willing to get out of your comfort zone in order to do God's will? Are you prepared to be scared?

John Cooper

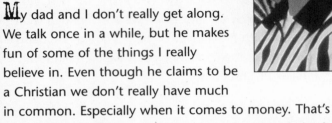

My dad and I don't really get along. We talk once in a while, but he makes fun of some of the things I really believe in. Even though he claims to be a Christian we don't really have much in common. Especially when it comes to money. That's made being in Skillet a little tough on me. My dad values what he calls "being normal," and playing in Christian rock band is not "normal" to him. To my dad, "normal" means doing anything with your life that makes a lot of money.

> No one can serve two masters. Either he will hate the one and love the other, or he will be devoted to the one and despise the other. You cannot serve both God and Money.
>
> Matthew 6:24

Dad doesn't think that playing in Skillet is working for a living. But it's not just being a Christian musician that bugs him. When I told him that I was going to go to college to become a schoolteacher, he just shook his head and said, "John, teachers don't make any money." It hurts that my dad doesn't support what I'm doing now. I know the only thing I could do that would make him happy would be to quit the band and become a doctor or lawyer or follow some other path that would make a lot of money.

Of course, he'd probably think differently about Skillet if we suddenly started making a zillion bucks, but in the real world of Christian music that's probably not going to happen. Still, deep in my heart I know I'm doing what I'm supposed to. Doing God's will is way more important than making money. Strength from that knowledge will have to be enough until God does something in my dad's life that brings him around.

What Did Jesus Do?

A certain ruler asked him, "Good teacher, what must I do to inherit eternal life?"

"Why do you call me good?" Jesus answered. "No one is good—except God alone. You know the commandments: 'Do not commit adultery, do not murder, do not steal, do not give false testimony, honor your father and mother.'

"All these I have kept since I was a boy," he said.

When Jesus heard this, he said to him, "You still lack one thing. Sell everything you have and give to the poor, and you will have treasure in heaven. Then come, follow me."

When he heard this, he became very sad, because he was a man of great wealth. Jesus looked at him and said, "How hard it is for the rich to enter the kingdom of God! Indeed, it is easier for a camel to go through the eye of a needle than for a rich man to enter the kingdom of God."

Those who heard this asked, "Who then can be saved?"

"Jesus replied, "What is impossible with men is possible with God."

Peter said to him, "We have left all we had to follow you!"

"I tell you the truth," Jesus said to them, "no one who has left home or wife or brothers or parents or children for the sake of the kingdom of God will fail to receive many times as much in this age and, in the age to come, eternal life." (Luke 18:18–30)

The Point!

Charles had just graduated from Bible college and taken a position as pastor at a rural Arkansas church. Even though the congregation was mostly made up of farmers who cared little about fashion, Charles felt it was important to look nice when he preached his first Sunday morning sermon.

The problem was Charles was broke. He couldn't afford a necktie, much less a whole suit.

A local funeral director had previously offered to give Charles any suit from his mortuary rack, and Charles decided he would take him up on his generosity. He went to the mortuary and picked out a beautiful gray suit that fit him perfectly. While he was admiring himself in the washroom mirror he reached to his pocket to retrieve a comb. Charles was startled to discover that funeral home suits don't have pockets—the folks wearing them don't have much use for pockets! To put it another way, "hearses don't pull U-hauls."

Jesus taught us to store treasure in heaven. If this life were all we had to hope for, He might well have said, "Don't be stupid. Make as much money as you can, kiddo, 'cause this life is all you've got." But Jesus taught us to always make our choices with heaven in mind. After all, we are only here for a second, but we'll be there for eternity.

 # What Should You Do?

What are the five most important things in your life?

Which of these five, if any, will make the trip to heaven with you?

When your life is coming to an end, what kind of things would you like to say you accomplished?

Danny Stephens

SMALLTOWN POETS

Yesterday I had to make a phone call to console an old friend whose dad had passed away. Cathy's dad was only fifty-five, but he died of cancer. It was a pretty tough pill for the family to swallow because they were under the impression that the cancer was in remission and he was getting better.

Cathy's dad was the pastor of Eastside Baptist; in fact, he had been my pastor for several years. So I knew that by now Cathy had heard every possible Christian cliché about losing a loved one. You know, things like, "He's in a better place now" and "We don't understand why, but someday in heaven we will." All those things are true, but I knew she would still be hurting inside.

I don't know what to do to ease your mind
I don't have the perfect word to make it fine
I'm not so qualified for sympathy
Still I am not without love
Psalm number four falls on your grieving ear
Yes, I believe the peace of Christ is near
And I am here in his name
You'd do the same, you'd do the same
If you'll let me close ... closer than a brother
If you'll let me love you ... we'll sit here and cry
Never failing, ever hoping
Seeking to preserve
It always is giving
Often without words
And when there's nothing left to say
Love has a voice
In sorrow and in heartache
There's a greater joy

"If You'll Let Me Love You"
Smalltown Poets

I had no idea what I was going to say to her. When she picked up the phone I just blurted out, "Cathy, I can't imagine what you must be going through right now. And I don't have any great pearls of wisdom to make you feel better and I sure can't bring your dad back, but I just wanted you to know that I really love you. And I'm hurting with you." After a slight pause, Cathy said, "Danny, that's enough, thanks. I love you, too."

Sometimes there aren't any magic fixes or clever words. Sometimes all you can do is wrap your arms around a friend and sit right there and cry.

What Would Jesus Do?

And many Jews had come to Martha and Mary to comfort them in the loss of their brother. When Martha heard that Jesus was coming, she went out to meet him, but Mary stayed at home.

"Lord," Martha said to Jesus, "if you had been here, my brother would not have died. But I know that even now God will give you whatever you ask."

Jesus said to her, "Your brother will rise again." Martha answered, "I know he will rise again in the resurrection at the last day."

Jesus said to her, "I am the resurrection and the life. He who believes in me will live, even though he dies; and whoever lives and believes in me will never die. Do you believe this?"

"Yes, Lord," she told him, "I believe that you are the Christ, the Son of God, who was to come into the world."

And after she had said this, she went back and called her sister Mary aside. "The Teacher is here," she said, "and is asking for you." When Mary heard this, she got up quickly and went to him. Now Jesus had not yet entered the village, but was still at the place where Martha had met him. When the Jews who had been with Mary in the house, comforting her, noticed how quickly she got up and went out, they followed her, supposing she was going to the tomb to mourn there.

When Mary reached the place where Jesus was and saw him, she fell at his feet and said, "Lord, if you had been here, my brother would not have died."

When Jesus saw her weeping, and the Jews who had come along with her also weeping, he was deeply moved in spirit and troubled. "Where have you laid him?" he asked.

"Come and see, Lord," they replied.

Jesus wept. (John 11:19–35)

 # The Point!

We live in a macho world where many men are afraid to show their emotions. They are taught that big boys don't cry, so when life deals them a crushing blow they are forced to put on a mask and pretend to be strong.

This is really unfortunate on two fronts. First of all, tears play an essential part in helping people deal with grief. Crying is not only a normal response to pain, it is the most healthy reaction. Research shows that holding grief in is very self-destructive, both emotionally and physically.

Second, a shared tear may be all the real consolation you have to give. Preparing a hot meal or offering a nugget of wisdom is always nice, but nothing helps heal an injured friend better than knowing that they are not shouldering their burden all alone. And nothing communicates this message with more eloquence than your tears.

What Should You Do?

How did you respond the last time you had a friend in pain?

How do you deal with tragedy? Are you afraid to show emotion?

Who in your life today do you need to tell that you love them?

Geoff Moore

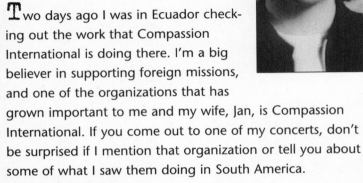

Two days ago I was in Ecuador checking out the work that Compassion International is doing there. I'm a big believer in supporting foreign missions, and one of the organizations that has grown important to me and my wife, Jan, is Compassion International. If you come out to one of my concerts, don't be surprised if I mention that organization or tell you about some of what I saw them doing in South America.

Blessed are the meek, for they will inherit the earth.
Blessed are those who hunger and thirst for righteousness, for they will be filled.
Blessed are the merciful, for they will be shown mercy.
Blessed are the pure in heart, for they will see God.

Matthew 5:5–8

Before I left the States, I had determined that I was going to find a new child to sponsor. But when the last day of the trip came around, I still hadn't picked out a child. I guess I was waiting for lightening to strike or something, but they were all so beautiful, dirty, and helpless. I just couldn't choose.

Well, we were visiting a little Salvation Army mission in the city of Quito. A group of precious young kids came out and sang to us and I decided to choose a child to sponsor from among them. After they sang, I sat down in the middle of about fifteen of the most affectionate kids I had ever seen. I asked one of coordinators to check which of these kids needed a sponsor. It was kind of strange because the coordinators kept asking me things like: "What age would I like? Would I prefer a girl or a boy?" It sounded more like buying a car. I told them, "I just want the child with the most need."

They came back and pointed to this gangly looking little boy sitting by himself. He was just ten years old, but he was three feet taller than everybody else. I was a little disappointed. I was thinking, "Oh man, I want one of these cute little cuddly kids." And then it dawned on me how selfish I was being. My feelings of disappointment indicted me. My charity and benevolence were somehow still intertwined with values that come from the world, not from Christ. Even though I was doing the right thing, it was clearly still linked to my own selfish agenda.

I went over to the boy to tell him I wanted to become his Compassion sponsor. I am so glad I did. I found out that guys his size and age have a great deal of difficulty getting help. It seems that, like me, most people want to help the smaller, cuter children. While his younger brother and sister had no trouble finding help, until now he had been overlooked.

I guess the lesson I learned through this is to keep a close eye on my motivation even when I'm doing the right thing. I think more often than we would hope, our motives are mixed with some of the selfishness left over from our old, sinful nature. It's quite possible to do good things, yet for all the wrong reasons.

What Did Ananias Do?

Now a man named Ananias, together with his wife Sapphira, also sold a piece of property. With his wife's full knowledge he kept back part of the money for himself, but brought the rest and put it at the apostles' feet.

Then Peter said, "Ananias, how is it that Satan has so filled your heart that you have lied to the Holy Spirit and have kept for yourself some of the money you received for the land? Didn't it belong to you before it was sold? And after it was sold, wasn't the money at your disposal? What made you think of doing such a thing? You have not lied to men but to God."

When Ananias heard this, he fell down and died. And great fear seized all who heard what had happened. Then the young men came forward, wrapped up his body, and carried him out and buried him.

About three hours later his wife came in, not knowing what had happened. Peter asked her, "Tell me, is this the price you and Ananias got for the land?"

"Yes," she said, "that is the price."

Peter said to her, "How could you agree to test the Spirit of the Lord? Look! The feet of the men who buried your husband are at the door, and they will carry you out also."

At that moment she fell down at his feet and died. Then the young men came in and, finding her dead, carried her out and buried her beside her husband. (Acts 5:1–10)

The Point!

A very respected minister was taking a walk through our neighborhood when he noticed a young boy struggling to push a doorbell. The boy would jump as high as he could, but he was just too short. So the minister, being a good Samaritan, walked over and pushed the doorbell for him. The pastor looked down at the boy and asked, "What now?" As the little boy turned into a blur he shouted over his shoulder, "Run like crazy!"

Appearances often deceive us because we can't see behind the veneer. Consequently, we are caught by surprise when a pillar of the community turns out to be a crook or when a pastor runs off with the church secretary. What if they were never caught? They might go on living as our role models and mentors. These are people we call hypocrites. But before you start your sermon, keep this in mind.

Very little (if any) of the good that people do is totally free from mixed motives. We may be giving that selfless sacrifice to God and country, but down deep, you know there is something in it for you, however tiny.

But guess what? God has the X-ray eyes of Superman. He sees our deeds and he knows our hearts. He weighs our thoughts. He not only knows everything that we do, he knows why we do it.

What Should You Do?

What is one thing in your life that no one knows about, that makes you feel like a hypocrite? Can you confess it to God right now?

Is there anyone or any group of people that you look down on? Who?

Do you make sure certain people know when you've done a good deed? Why or why not?

Pete Stewart

GRAMMATRAIN

One of the hardest choices I've ever had to make was when grammatrain started to take off. I have wanted to play in a Christian band all my life, but when it really came time to make the leap, a lot of sacrifice was involved. If you're going to really make a go of a Christian music career, you've got to get on the road and do it full time.

For my wife and me that meant moving out of our house and putting most of our stuff in storage. We've basically had to live out of a suitcase for the last year and a half. It's kind of stressful when we do have some time off to come back to Seattle and stay with either friends or family. Right now, we are staying with my parents, and that can be tough. I love my parents dearly, and they're probably the easiest parents in the world to live with, but I'm married now and it seems a little strange at times to be at their house instead of our own.

The biggest thing my wife, Donna, and I miss is privacy. When you're on tour privacy doesn't exist. And sometimes we are out for five months straight. So, for months you are with

> Peter answered him, "We have left everything to follow you! What then will there be for us?"
> Jesus said to them, "I tell you the truth, at the renewal of all things, when the Son of Man sits on his glorious throne, you who have followed me will also sit on twelve thrones, judging the twelve tribes of Israel. And everyone who has left houses or brothers or sisters or father or mother or children or fields for my sake will receive a hundred times as much and will inherit eternal life."
>
> Matthew 19:27–29

people twenty-four hours a day. You're out there thinking, "I can't wait to get back to that nice little home and get a some time to myself." And then you realize, "Oh yeah! I don't have a home."

The thing that makes all of this okay, though, is that deep down we know that we are doing what God wants us to do. And we are seeing results. There is nothing else more satisfying than using your gifts in his service. Just this past weekend, at a show, a girl handed me a letter saying that the last time we were in North Carolina a friend brought her to the concert. She had become a Christian that night and wanted us to know how much our ministry meant to her. No amount of money, houses, or fame could ever match the feeling I have when I read letters like that one. A letter or two like that makes it worth all the inconveniences.

What Would Jesus Do?

As they were walking along the road, a man said to him, "I will follow you wherever you go."

Jesus replied, "Foxes have holes and birds of the air have nests, but the Son of Man has no place to lay his head."

He said to another man, "Follow me."

But the man replied, "Lord, first let me go and bury my father."

Jesus said to him, "Let the dead bury their own dead, but you go and proclaim the kingdom of God."

Still another said, "I will follow you, Lord; but first let me go back and say good-by to my family."

Jesus replied, "No one who puts his hand to the plow and looks back is fit for service in the kingdom of God. (Luke 9:57–62)

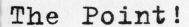

The Point!

David Livingstone was one of the most famous missionar-ies of modern times. In his journal he once said, "People talk of the sacrifices I have made in spending so much of my life in Africa. Can that be called a sacrifice which is simply paying back a small part of the great debt owing to our God, which we can never repay? Is that a sacrifice which brings its own blest reward in healthful activity, the consciousness of doing good, peace of mind and a bright hope of a glorious destiny hereafter? Away with the word in such a view and with such a thought! It is emphatically no sacrifice. Say rather it is a privilege" (*Giving and Living* by Samuel Young, Baker Book House, p.71).

A wealthy southern gentleman who reportedly gave 90 percent of his income to God was asked by a curious reporter how he found the strength to part with so much. The gentleman told him, "Sir, the only part of my income that I'm parting with is the 10 percent I spend on me. The rest of it is an investment in my future and I expect to see it again."

What Should You Do?

If God asked you to leave your home for the mission field, would you do it?

Would it be harder to part with friends, family, or your possessions?

Do you give some portion your time and money to God? What can you do to increase that portion?

Todd Kirby

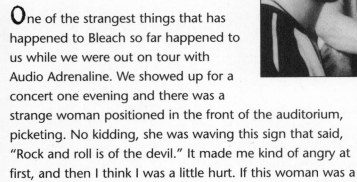

One of the strangest things that has happened to Bleach so far happened to us while we were out on tour with Audio Adrenaline. We showed up for a concert one evening and there was a strange woman positioned in the front of the auditorium, picketing. No kidding, she was waving this sign that said, "Rock and roll is of the devil." It made me kind of angry at first, and then I think I was a little hurt. If this woman was a Christian, I thought she was supposed to be on our side. I mean, we were out there telling people about Jesus, and to be honest, we were struggling to get by. I guess we just assumed religious people would be supportive, whether they dug our music or not.

Thankfully, nobody lost it. We all just kind of took a deep breath and decided the best thing to do was just to sit down and talk to her in a Christlike way. She started out saying God had told her we were doing something wrong and that she needed to stand out there and warn people. Then Sam asked her, "What do you think God has been saying to all the people who have been praying for this concert for months? Don't you think that all of the churches, the pastors, and youth pastors who have made this concert happen are listening to God's voice too?" Good question, but still we hit a stone wall.

> *Blessed are those who are persecuted because of righteousness, for theirs is the kingdom of heaven. Blessed are you when people insult you, persecute you and falsely say all kinds of evil against you because of me. Rejoice and be glad, because great is your reward in heaven, for in the same way they persecuted the prophets who were before you.*
>
> *Matthew 5:10–12*

She wanted to talk about the "evil" birth of rock and roll and how it was not a suitable medium for sharing the gospel. We told her something we learned in Bible college. Many of our favorite hymns, like "A Mighty Fortress Is Our God," started out as bar tunes that somebody put Christian lyrics to. Even our own national anthem was a bar tune. The original songs have been transformed through time. How we look at rock music has changed through the years, too.

In the end she went her way and we played our concert. I don't think much of what we said ever broke through to her. But my hope is that she at least thought long and hard about our attitudes toward her. I mean, it was the first time that Bleach had been told to our faces that we were from the devil, and by the grace of God, we were able to react in a way that wasn't counterproductive. If she couldn't hear Jesus in our music, maybe she could at least get a glimpse of him in the way we acted toward her.

What Would Jesus Do?

"I am sending you out like sheep among wolves. Therefore be as shrewd as snakes and as innocent as doves. Be on your guard against men; they will hand you over to the local councils and flog you in their synagogues. On my account you will be brought before governors and kings as witnesses to them and to the Gentiles. But when they arrest you, do not worry about what to say or how to say it. At that time you will be given what to say, for it will not be you speaking, but the Spirit of your Father speaking through you.

"Brother will betray brother to death, and a father his child; children will rebel against their parents and have them put to death. All men will hate you because of me, but he who stands firm to the end will be saved.

"When you are persecuted in one place, flee to another. I tell you the truth, you will not finish going through the cities of Israel before the Son of Man comes.

"A student is not above his teacher, nor a servant above his master. It is enough for the student to be like his teacher, and the servant like his master. If the head of the house has been called Beelzebub, how much more the members of his household!" (Matthew 10:16–25)

The Point!

Hundreds of years before the birth of Christ, the prophet Isaiah predicted than when the Messiah came he would be called Wonderful Counselor, Mighty God, Everlasting Father, and Prince of Peace (Isaiah 9:6). Later when Jesus was actually born, the angels proclaimed, "Glory to God in the highest, and on earth peace to men" (Luke 2:14).

So, where is the peace? It seems that Jesus taught his disciples to go into the world expecting anything but peace. Peace isn't out there in the world. For many of you, it won't even be in your own family. The peace that Christ brings is experienced on the inside. It's a quiet refreshing of the soul that whispers that, no matter what happens, Jesus loves you and he is always near.

Some people can't understand the peace of Christ because they confuse happiness with peace. Peace and happiness are not the same. Happiness is what you feel based on what takes place in the external world. It is at the total mercy of happenstance. My girlfriend loves me—I feel happy; I've got a giant zit on prom night—I'm depressed.

Peace is only subject to one variable. Is Jesus here? Where Jesus is, there is peace, and if the Prince of Peace lives in your heart, you can experience perfect peace in any circumstance.

So what's the point? It's simply this: As we go about the business of serving God out there in the real world, there will be many days that make us feel happy. But other days it will seem that even our own families have turned against us. Yet our peace does not depend upon them. It is not that fragile or changeable. Our peace has a faithful source. It flows from a river within our hearts where the Prince of Peace makes his home.

 # What Should You Do?

How far do we need to go in order to get along with those who disagree with us? When does peacemaking become compromising?

Which of your beliefs might make you unpopular at school or work?

Would you speak out for Jesus if it meant losing your friends? your freedom?

Brad Olsen

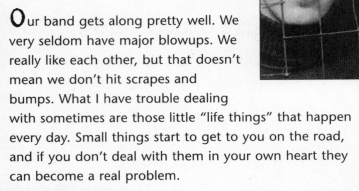

THE WAITING

Our band gets along pretty well. We very seldom have major blowups. We really like each other, but that doesn't mean we don't hit scrapes and bumps. What I have trouble dealing with sometimes are those little "life things" that happen every day. Small things start to get to you on the road, and if you don't deal with them in your own heart they can become a real problem.

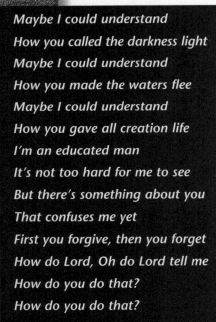

Maybe I could understand
How you called the darkness light
Maybe I could understand
How you made the waters flee
Maybe I could understand
How you gave all creation life
I'm an educated man
It's not too hard for me to see
But there's something about you
That confuses me yet
First you forgive, then you forget
How do Lord, Oh do Lord tell me
How do you do that?
How do you do that?

"How Do You Do That?"
The Waiting

For instance, I usually end up rooming with Brandon, who for the most part is really easy to get along with. But sometimes Brandon will hit the shower first and take forever to get out. Just about the time he reappears all dressed and ready for the day, the road manager knocks on the door screaming, "Five minutes!" So I either have to set a world record for showering or face the day feeling grungy. I know this doesn't make Brandon the Unabomber, but after a couple of times it gets annoying.

I don't have a problem forgiving a person who messes up. We all mess up. But sometimes it takes me far too long to forget. I mean, sometimes I'll go into the shower first and I'll be thinking, "I'm gonna stay in here as long as I want and I don't care who misses their shower today."

I know it sounds childish, because it is. But a lot of our sin comes from that rebellious child within. I'm starting to see those "little life" things as great opportunities for me to make progress in growing up spiritually. Every day it seems I get a zillion chances to practice a skill that my heavenly Father has obviously mastered: I get the chance to learn how to forgive *and* forget. So I guess I should thank Brandon for helping out … but get out of the shower!

What Would Jesus Do?

Jesus straightened up and asked her, "Woman, where are they? Has no one condemned you?"

"No one, sir," she said.

"Then neither do I condemn you," Jesus declared. "Go now and leave your life of sin." (John 8:10–11)

Some men brought to him a paralytic, lying on a mat. When Jesus saw their faith, he said to the paralytic, "Take heart, son; your sins are forgiven." (Matthew 9:2)

Then Jesus said to her, "Your sins are forgiven." (Luke 7:48)

Jesus said, "Father, forgive them, for they do not know what they are doing." And they divided up his clothes by casting lots. (Luke 23:34)

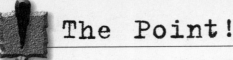

The Point!

Life holds a lot of great mysteries. Simply put, there are some things we weren't meant to understand. Like why do we park in a driveway and drive on a parkway? Or if I'm driving some night at the speed of light and turn on my headlights, am I going to be able to see anything? And where do my socks go when they disappear in the dryer? Also, why did kamikazes wear helmets? (Think about it.)

I heard a man tell a new convert that the Bible has the answer to everything, but that's not exactly true. There are some mysteries that go unexplained. One of the greatest mysteries of all is the forgetfulness of God. How is it that the intellect that designed the universe somehow fails when it comes to remembering our sins? How is it that a God who knows the length of every pine needle on every pine tree in Colorado can't keep up with the record of our failures? I heard an old country gentleman preach on this topic once. And when he finished reading the verses about God's forgetfulness he said, "I don't understand a thing I just said to you, but I believe every word." I think I agree.

I guess the best explanation I've heard is that somewhere among God's infinite list of amazing talents ought to be one called "selective amnesia." We ask him, "But Lord, what about my sin?" It's this divine ability that allows him to answer, "What sin?"

What Should You Do?

Describe one thing in your past that you think God is holding against you.

Describe one thing from your past that you are holding against someone else.

God has promised to forgive *and forget* our sins. Do you really, deep down believe this?

Pearl Barrett

I want to be real, I want to be real
Don't want to be a fake, no imitation situation
I want to be real, I want to be real
I really want to be real
To tell the truth
I haven't always stood for where I stand
There were times I could have testified
But my head was in the sand
Like Peter I never thought I could deny him at all
* (but you never know)*
You never know you're going to fall until you fall
I've got this little tendency to blend into the crowd
I've pretended to be saintly,
* even tried to be profound.*
Laughed just like a sinner when my heart knew
* it was wrong*
God I need some help cause
* I'm just dying to be strong*
The masquerade is over, identity revealed
And just like I told you,
* I'm going to stand for truth*
And it's going to be real

"Real"
Considering Lily

I've never been to public school in America because Serene and I grew up in Australia.

We hear about guns and drugs in schools in America. It must be tough to walk with the Lord while going to public high school here, but I think it was just as tough in Australia for different reasons. In Australia less than 5 percent of the population go to church. I mean any church. People are proud to tell you they're atheists. It's as if they think it makes them intellectually superior. That's a difficult environment to thrive in, especially for a pastor's daughter.

I remember one day at school we were asked to go around the room and tell what our fathers did for a living. I love my dad and I'm very proud of him, but I was nervous when my turn came. The teacher said, "So, Pearl, tell us what your dad does for a living."

Sheepishly I said, "He's a minister and I go to his church." People actually laughed out loud. I wanted to crawl under my desk.

I didn't say anything about Jesus for a long time after that. Sometimes I would have the perfect opportunity to speak up and I wouldn't. I can't tell how sad it made me. I was really disappointed with myself for a long time.

Then I met Tina. Tina wasn't a Christian, but she became one of my best friends. I grew to trust her with my feelings because she accepted me as I was. Looking back, Tina wouldn't have cared if I was a Christian, an atheist, or a Buddhist monk. She had her own problems to worry about.

Tina's parents were going through a nasty divorce, and I think that's one of the reasons she became anorexic. I realized that, for Tina's sake, I had to get up the courage to tell her about Jesus. And I did. It was a wonderful feeling to finally be sharing my faith. Telling one person about Christ may seem like a small thing, but for me it was huge. It was one of those things that you can build on. Had I remained silent, I may have never have gained the daily courage I need now to share Christ through the ministry of Considering Lily.

What Would Jesus Do?

He went to Nazareth, where he had been brought up, and on the Sabbath day he went into the synagogue, as was his custom. And he stood up to read. The scroll of the prophet Isaiah was handed to him. Unrolling it, he found the place where it is written: "The Spirit of the Lord is on me, because he has anointed me to preach good news to the poor. He has sent me to proclaim freedom for the prisoners and recovery of sight for the blind, to release the oppressed, to proclaim the year of the Lord's favor." Then he rolled up the scroll, gave it back to the attendant and sat down.

The eyes of everyone in the synagogue were fastened on him, and he began by saying to them, "Today this scripture is fulfilled in your hearing."

All spoke well of him and were amazed at the gracious words that came from his lips. "Isn't this Joseph's son?" they asked.

Jesus said to them, "Surely you will quote this proverb to me: 'Physician, heal yourself! Do here in your hometown what we have heard that you did in Capernaum.'"

"I tell you the truth," he continued, "no prophet is accepted in his hometown." (Luke 4:16–24)

The Point!

One of the very last instructions Jesus gave his disciples was this: "You will receive power when the Holy Spirit comes on you; and you will be my witnesses in Jerusalem, and in all Judea and Samaria, and to the ends of the earth" (Acts 1:8). Many believe the order of the cities mentioned by Jesus were no accident. This could be a strategic blueprint for personal evangelism.

If you look at a Bible map of Israel during Jesus' day, you'll find that each of the places mentioned are just a bit farther out from the starting place, Jerusalem. The disciples are told to be witnesses first where they are. Then they are to move out a little farther to Judea. When they've done with that, they are instructed to move out again until finally they are witnessing in outer Mongolia.

The problem is that when Jesus told them this, it had only been slightly more than a month since they crucified Jesus right there in Jerusalem. I'm sure some of the disciples were thinking, "Lord, couldn't we start with the ends of the Earth and work our way back to town when things are safe?"

Not a chance. Jesus wanted them to start where it would be the hardest, right where they were.

For most people it's easier to witness to total strangers than to their own family. It can be intimidating to share your faith in your own home, at your school, or where you work. Who cares what a stranger thinks about your faith? More than likely you will never see the person again. But the people where you live know who you really are, and deep down you care what they think. Maybe you care too much. Would you rather be liked or see your friends go to heaven?

What Should You Do?

Who among your friends really need to hear about Jesus?

Who among your family members need to hear about Christ? (Don't forget aunts, uncles, and cousins.)

What will you tell them? When?

John Cooper

SKILLET

People back in high school always thought of me as being radical for God. What they didn't know was that I didn't really know God at all. I was very religious, I kept the rules, but I didn't have a real connection with Jesus Christ. I wasn't trying to be a hypocrite—I had as much of a relationship as I knew how. I even talked to some of my friends about Jesus and some of them got saved. But I really didn't know what being a Christian was all about.

> *Woe to you, teachers of the law and Pharisees, you hypocrites! You are like whitewashed tombs, which look beautiful on the outside but on the inside are full of dead men's bones and everything unclean.*
>
> *Matthew 23:27*

I never did drugs, drank, or had sex, but still I was a long way from having a living, breathing friendship with Jesus. None of my friends knew how really dead my spiritual life was at that time because I didn't even know myself.

This is going to sound weird, but it wasn't until my mother got sick with cancer that I discovered how far I really was from God. My mom was the first of our family to discover that being religious wasn't the same as knowing Christ. She was searching to find healing from her cancer, or at least for some kind of meaning in it. She was praying and reading her Bible like never before. She decided to go looking for a church that could feed her new appetite for Jesus. When she found one, I went with her.

Over the course of the next year, we went through a lot of ups and downs. We had to deal with Mom's chemotherapy and illness. At the same time, she and I were really growing in the Spirit. I loved my mom a lot and even though we eventually lost her, because of her I found a living connection to Christ that's growing every day. Now that I've experienced the fullness of Christ, I will never again settle for mere empty religion.

What Did Jesus Do?

Then Jesus said to the crowds and to his disciples. "The teachers of the law and the Pharisees sit in Moses' seat. So you must obey them and do everything they tell you. But do not do what they do, for they do not practice what they preach....

"Woe to you, teachers of the law and Pharisees, you hypocrites! You are like whitewashed tombs, which look beautiful on the outside but on the inside are full of dead men's bones and everything unclean. In the same way, on the outside you appear to people as righteous but on the inside you are full of hypocrisy and wickedness.

"Woe to you, teachers of the law and Pharisees, you hypocrites! You build tombs for the prophets and decorate the graves of the righteous. You snakes! You brood of vipers! How will you escape being condemned to hell?" (Matthew 23:1–3, 27–33)

The Point!

When Jesus met Zacchaeus, the crooked tax collector, he asked to be invited to dinner. When he came across a hardened group of rough fishermen he said, "Come and follow me." When he spoke to the woman caught in adultery he said, "Go and sin no more." But when Jesus ran into the ultra-religious Pharisees, he called them "snakes" and "vipers" and warned them that they were on their way to hell. Why would Jesus speak so harshly to the Pharisees?

It's not only that they were trying to earn their way into heaven by doing good things, but that they were teaching others to do the same. The Bible tells us that we are saved by God's grace alone (Ephesians 2:8). The reason God may have chosen this way to save us is that it is probably the only way possible.

From a vantage point anchored to our small human existence, the moral distance between some people appears to be incredibly wide. Some stand tall while others look like moral midgets. Hitler looks like a demon deserving of hell; Billy Graham looks like a giant who could touch heaven from his tiptoes. This kind of moral scale makes good sense when we are comparing ourselves to ourselves. The problem is that in order to get a free pass to heaven you have to compare yourself to a pure and holy God.

Suppose you have been training for the Olympic high jump competition. You arrive on game day to discover that to qualify you have to make a minimum height. Not to worry, you're jumping against an old fat guy and a woman in a wheelchair. Sure, you can soar above your competition, but that's not your problem. The real problem is that the bar for making the minimum qualifying height is set at the moon. You'll look pretty awesome against an old fat guy and a woman in a wheelchair, but the distance you outjump them is only a tiny fraction of what you need to clear the moon.

If you are trusting your goodness alone to qualify you for that leap into heaven, you're going to come up painfully short. From God's point of view, only perfect obedience will launch you to heaven—even one half of one sin will keep you out. Jesus is the only human being who was able to make that moral leap, and if you're planning getting there yourself, you'd better grab His coattails and hang on!

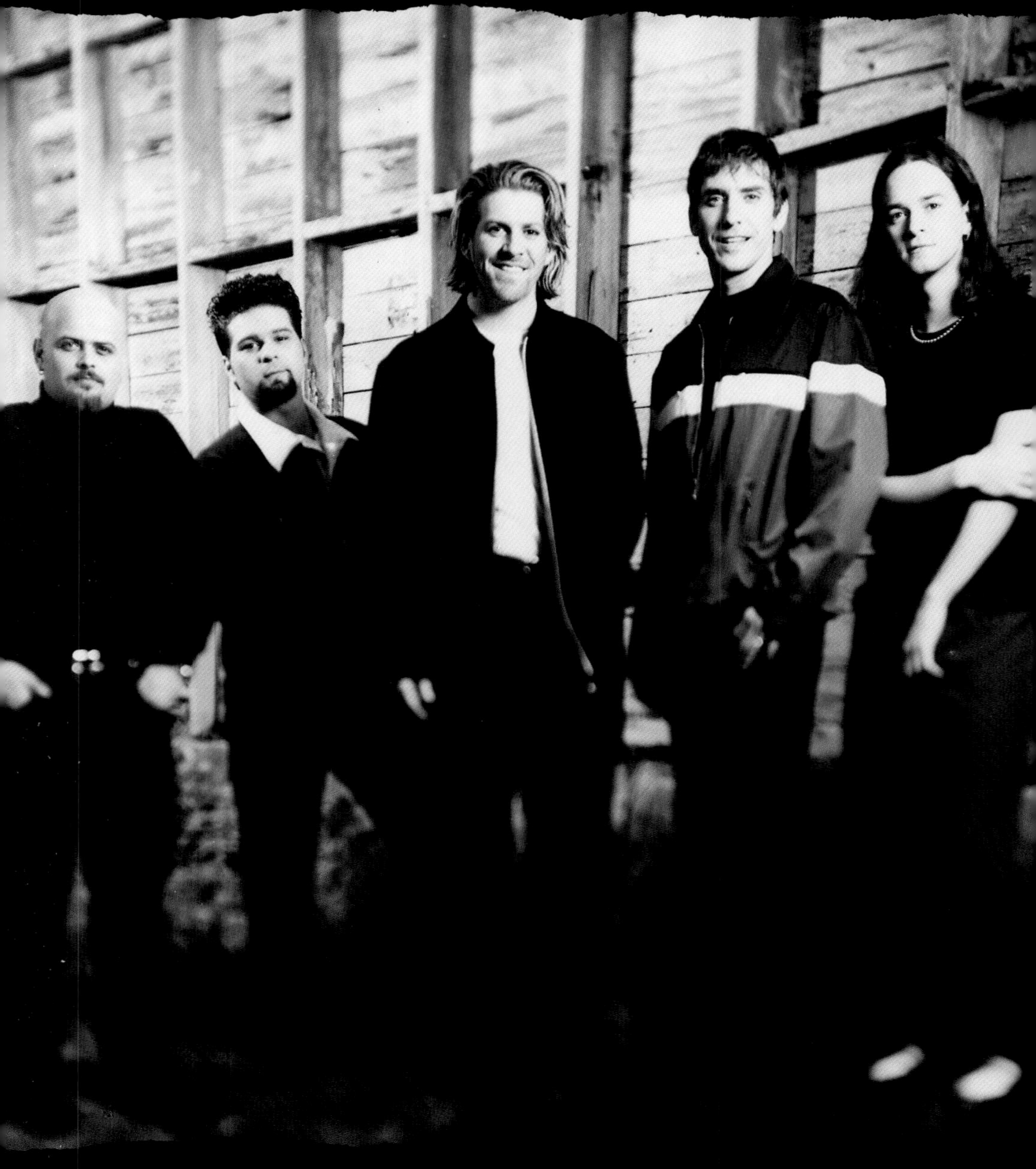

Rebecca St. James

Smalltown Poets

Skillet

Audio Adrenaline

The Waiting

Steven Curtis Chapman

dana key

What Should You Do?

Do you believe that God will be persuaded to let you into heaven because you are a good person?

If being good won't get you into heaven, why should you keep trying to be good?

Have you ever asked Jesus to come into your life and to be your personal Savior? If not, are you willing to take that step today?

Do you have the kind of friendship with Jesus that makes you want to talk to him every day?

Will McGinniss

AUDIO ADRENALINE

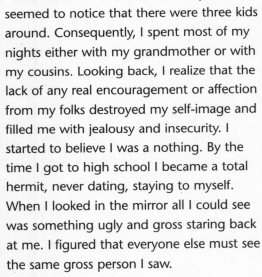

I grew up in a family setting that was totally weird, totally terrible. My mom had married three different people before I was twelve. There was never really a father figure in my life. My mom and her husbands were focused on themselves; they never seemed to notice that there were three kids around. Consequently, I spent most of my nights either with my grandmother or with my cousins. Looking back, I realize that the lack of any real encouragement or affection from my folks destroyed my self-image and filled me with jealousy and insecurity. I started to believe I was a nothing. By the time I got to high school I became a total hermit, never dating, staying to myself. When I looked in the mirror all I could see was something ugly and gross staring back at me. I figured that everyone else must see the same gross person I saw.

If it weren't for my cousin Thad and his family, who knows where I'd be now— probably dead. But they were so good to me. They never judged me; instead, they made me feel like one of their family. They included me in everything, even in their church. And their church was a special place. The people there were like Thad's family: loving and caring. I felt accepted for the first time. It didn't take long for me to realize that the love and accep-

> *Sing to God, sing praise to his name, extol him who rides on the clouds— his name is the Lord—and rejoice before him. A father to the fatherless, a defender of widows, is God in his holy dwelling. God sets the lonely in families, he leads forth the prisoners with singing; but the rebellious live in a sun-scorched land.*
>
> *Psalm 68:4–6*

tance they were showing me was just a reflection of the love and acceptance that each of them had discovered in Jesus Christ. These people were Jesus to me, a geeky kid who most people wouldn't have looked at twice.

Because of the way they treated me, when their pastor sat me down one day and read me some scriptures that explained God's love and forgiveness, I was ready to ask Jesus into my life. Suddenly I didn't feel like a nothing anymore. It means a lot to know that I was valuable enough that my Father in heaven gave up His only Son to die for me. Jesus has performed a miracle on my broken heart, and I've finally found the Father figure I never had.

What Would Jesus Do?

So he came to a town in Samaria called Sychar, near the plot of ground Jacob had given to his son Joseph. Jacob's well was there, and Jesus, tired as he was from the journey, sat down by the well. It was about the sixth hour.

When a Samaritan woman came to draw water, Jesus said to her, "Will you give me a drink?" (His disciples had gone into the town to buy food.) The Samaritan woman said to him, "You are a Jew and I am a Samaritan woman. How can you ask me for a drink?" (For Jews do not associate with Samaritans.)

Jesus answered her, "If you knew the gift of God and who it is that asks you for a drink, you would have asked him and he would have given you living water. ... Everyone who drinks this water will be thirsty again, but whoever drinks the water I give him will never thirst. Indeed, the water I give him will become in him a spring of water welling up to eternal life." (John 4:5–10, 13–14)

The Point!

Jesus met a woman who because of her bad reputation was forced to retrieve water by herself in the hottest part of the day. Jesus had every reason to avoid this woman like the plague. She had three strikes against her.

Strike one: The Samaritan's were viewed as racially inferior outcasts by many of the Jewish people.

Strike two: This was a woman who had been married five times and was presently living with a man who was not her husband.

Strike three: She was a woman. Keep in mind that many men at this time viewed women as property. To some men her value could be measured in donkeys, horses, or animal skins, but not to Jesus.

The good news is that Jesus doesn't see us like others do. He doesn't even see us like we see ourselves. Like Thad, his family, and the people at his church, Jesus has the kind of vision that sees beyond the external. When Jesus looked upon the woman at the well he saw a damaged heart in need of eternal forgiveness.

What Should You Do?

Who do you know who feels like a geek? In what ways could you include that person in your life and church?

Do you believe that you are special enough to God that He would be willing to send His Son to die for just you? Why or why not?

Steve Wiggins

The other day we had a fourteen-hour bus trip ahead of us and I started to think about what was I going to do with all that time. I love to read, but not for fourteen straight hours. Then it occurred to me to just tape shows off of TV, but you know, there just aren't fourteen hours of worthwhile television available. There aren't even four. Should I rent some movies? If so, which ones? All of these questions eventually get back to how much will I compromise my standards to keep from being bored.

These are issues that people have to deal with every day. What am going to watch? What am I going to listen to? And once you start to compromise your standards, it's easier to do it the next time you're tested too.

I'm not a perfect guy. Sometimes I pass the test, but in all honesty, sometimes I don't. People might wonder how I can stand up on stage and say, "Hey, Buddy, you better wake up," or sing a song that says, "You'd better get it together spiritually." But I'm not pointing my finger at other people, I'm preaching to myself as well.

When I wrote "Where's The Passion" for our first record, I was writing about me. "I searched the land for a willing man and I found many. And one by one, the hard

> *For we do not have a high priest who is unable to sympathize with our weaknesses, but we have one who has been tempted in every way, just as we are—yet was without sin. Let us then approach the throne of grace with confidence, so that we may receive mercy and find grace to help us in our time of need.*
>
> Hebrews 4:15–16

times came and they all up and left Me." That's what Jesus was saying to me at the time. We are getting ready to put a song called "Come On People" on our new album. It's a song about getting out of your seat, off your duff, and into the world to share Christ. That's what I hear Jesus saying to me now. When I'm singing, I hope people will remember that I'm just passing along a secondhand sermon that the Holy Spirit has already preached to me first.

I hope everybody remembers that I'm still learning, I'm still grow-ing. I'm still striving to become the man of God I know he wants me to be. I know I'm not who I want to be yet, but then again, I'm not who I used to be either.

What Would Jesus Do?

Then Jesus was led by the Spirit into the desert to be tempted by the devil. After fasting forty days and forty nights, he was hungry. The tempter came to him and said, "If you are the Son of God, tell these stones to become bread." Jesus answered, "It is written: "Man does not live on bread alone, but on every word that comes from the mouth of God."

Then the devil took him to the holy city and had him stand on the highest point of the temple. "If you are the Son of God," he said, "throw yourself down. For it is written: "'He will command his angels concerning you, and they will lift you up in their hands, so that you will not strike your foot against a stone.'" Jesus answered him, "It is also written: 'Do not put the Lord your God to the test.'"

Again, the devil took him to a very high mountain and showed him all the kingdoms of the world and their splendor. "All this I will give you," he said, "if you will bow down and worship me." Jesus said to him, "Away from me, Satan! For it is written: 'Worship the Lord your God, and serve him only.'" Then the devil left him, and angels came and attended him. (Matthew 4:1–11)

The Point!

One of the things that helps us to have confidence when we go to God in prayer is the knowledge that Jesus has been tempted in every way that we have. He knows how it feels to be hungry, angry, lonely, jilted, or tempted to take a detour out of God's will.

Satan offered Jesus a way to be fed, to be famous, and to rule the world. Those of us who have skipped to the back of the book already know how the story ends for Jesus. We know that he will rule the world eventually. As we see Jesus being tempted by Satan out there in the wilderness, it makes you want to shout, "Don't fall for it, Jesus. You're going to rule the world someday, just hang tough!" Jesus must have known that what Satan was offering was his to own in the not-so-distant future. So where's the temptation? It is this: Satan's offer was a shortcut. It gave Jesus a kingdom that didn't include a cross.

Sometimes doing it God's way means doing it the hard way. God's will is sometimes the path of patience and sometimes the path of pain. But it is guaranteed by the unfailing promise of God that his will is always the path of perfect peace.

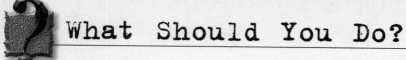

What Should You Do?

If you got home from the store and discovered you had been undercharged for something, would you go back and report it? Would the amount matter?

What kind of movies do you consider strictly out of bounds for you?

What are your "entertainment boundaries"? How much are you guided by what your friends do?

Michael Tait

Is this one for the people?

Is this one for the Lord?

Or do I simply serenade for things I
    must afford

You can jumble them together, my
    conflict still remains

For holiness is calling, in the midst
    of courting fame

'Cause I see the trust in their eyes

Though the sky is falling

They need your love in their lives

Compromise is calling

What if I stumble, what if I fall?

What if I lose my step and I make
    fools of us all

Will the love continue?

When my walk becomes a crawl

What if I stumble and what if I fall

I hear you whispering my name—you say

My love for you will never change,
    never change

"What If I Stumble?"
dc Talk

I think it's pretty common for people in the public eye to sometimes wonder about their audience and even about their friends. If I slip up will they support me? If the next record bombs are they gonna stick around? This might come as a surprise, but I'm as insecure as the next guy. Some people can't see past those bright lights of fame to realize that we musicians are vulnerable. They might think we can walk on water, but we can't.

I know some people think of us as role models, and that puts even more pressure on us to stay spiritually focused. Not that we don't accept that responsibility, but I wish more people understood that the world is watching all of us. Being called to be "the light of the world" makes every Christian into a role model for someone. And the other thing people should keep in mind is that we don't stand or fall based upon what anyone else thinks of us. We stand or fall based on what God thinks of our lives.

"What If I Stumble?" asks what are you going to do if someone around you takes a nose dive. The song is not some kind of a prediction. We're just saying that some already have fallen and it's not just people in Christian music. We've got injured Christians all around us. I heard a man say that the Army of God is the only army that shoots its own wounded. That's a shame. Jesus told us that we should be recognized for our love for one another.

God forbid that I stumble, but if I do, I hope you will be there for me. I'll do my best to be there for you, too.

What Did Peter Do?

Peter declared, "Even if all fall away, I will not."

"I tell you the truth," Jesus answered, "today—yes, tonight—before the rooster crows twice you yourself will disown me three times."

But Peter insisted emphatically, "Even if I have to die with you, I will never disown you." And all the others said the same....

While Peter was below in the courtyard, one of the servant girls of the high priest came by. When she saw Peter warming himself, she looked closely at him.

"You also were with that Nazarene, Jesus," she said.

But he denied it. "I don't know or understand what you're talking about," he said, and went out into the entryway.

When the servant girl saw him there, she said again to those standing around, "This fellow is one of them." Again he denied it.

After a little while, those standing near said to Peter, "Surely you are one of them, for you are a Galilean."

He began to call down curses on himself, and he swore to them, "I don't know this man you're talking about."

Immediately the rooster crowed the second time. Then Peter remembered the word Jesus had spoken to him: "Before the rooster crows twice you will disown me three times." And he broke down and wept. (Mark 14:29–31, 66–72)

The Point!

After Peter betrays Jesus you might expect the Bible to say, "and the next time Jesus ran into Peter, he called down lightening from the sky and all that was left of Peter was two smoking sandals." If I were God (and you should be thankful I'm not), that's probably how the story would have ended.

Instead, soon after Peter's three betrayals, Jesus cooks him breakfast, and the conversation between the two of them is not about Peter's failure that night, but rather it focuses on love and obedience. "When they had finished eating, Jesus said to Simon Peter, 'Simon son of John, do you truly love me more than these?' 'Yes, Lord,' he said, 'you know that I love you.' Jesus said, 'Feed my lambs'" (John 21:15).

I don't think it was a coincidence that Jesus asked this question three times. Jesus wasn't hard of hearing or difficult to convince. The repetition was for Peter's sake. It was as if each question washed away one of Peter's denials. Jesus already knew the answer to each of the questions. He didn't really need Peter to say he loved him three times. Jesus simply wanted Peter know with certainty that he was aware of Peter's true feelings and was gladly accepting Peter back into his service.

Peter got up from this breakfast appointment free and forgiven. He went out and rocked his world for Christ. I'll bet there are people around each of us that could do the same if we were as quick to forgive and willing to forget.

What Should You Do?

Do you have greater trouble forgiving some more than others? Who and why?

In what way has someone let you down, or even betrayed you?

Who looks to you as a role model?

Kevin Breuner

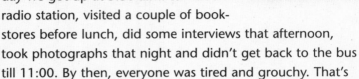

SMALLTOWN POETS

Lately we've been making a lot of publicity trips. These are some of the hardest days for me. I mean, the other day we got up at 5:30 a.m. to visit a radio station, visited a couple of bookstores before lunch, did some interviews that afternoon, took photographs that night and didn't get back to the bus till 11:00. By then, everyone was tired and grouchy. That's when I start to slip into my selfish mode, where I want my space or I just want something for me. You get tired of giving so much and you just want to start taking.

Bear with each other and forgive whatever grievances you may have against one another. Forgive as the Lord forgave you.

Colossians 3:13

It seems utterly stupid now, but when you're really tired the smallest things start to bug you. Someone will leave stuff in your private space or insist on watching a movie you've seen a billion times or just say something that rubs you the wrong way. I wish I could just let it go, but I have the tendency to sit and dwell on things. Even when someone asks for forgiveness, sometimes I feel it takes me longer than it should to give it up and say, "That's cool, don't worry about it."

That's one of the things I most admire about Jesus. There he is, this sinless guy with the most vile people you can imagine coming up to him wanting forgiveness. And without even thinking twice he says, "You're forgiven." Just like that, it's a done deal. The past is forgotten. I'd like to be more like that.

What Would Jesus Do?

So Pilate decided to grant their demand. He released the man who had been thrown into prison for insurrection and murder, the one they asked for, and surrendered Jesus to their will. As they led him away, they seized Simon from Cyrene, who was on his way in from the country, and put the cross on him and made him carry it behind Jesus. A large number of people followed him, including women who mourned and wailed for him.

Jesus turned and said to them, "Daughters of Jerusalem, do not weep for me; weep for yourselves and for your children."

Two other men, both criminals, were also led out with him to be executed. When they came to the place called the Skull, there they crucified him, along with the criminals—one on his right, the other on his left. Jesus said, "Father, forgive them, for they do not know what they are doing." And they divided up his clothes by casting lots. (Luke 23:24–34)

The Point!

Corrie ten Boom suffered horribly in a Nazi concentration camp during World War II. In her book, *The Hiding Place*, Corrie talks about, after her release, running into one of her former guards in a church in Munich in which she was speaking. After the service, the former soldier approached her with face gleaming. He said to her, "How grateful I am for your message, Fraulein. To think that, as you say, He has washed my sins away."

He raised his hand to shake hers, but Corrie couldn't. Her hand remained paralyzed at her side. All she could think of were the faces of those she had seen beaten, raped, and murdered. This was the same man who had mocked them as they were herded naked into the showers.

She prayed, "Lord Jesus, help me to forgive him." But still her hand did not move.

Even as she seethed with anger she thought, "Jesus died for this man, can I ask for more?"

Again she prayed, "Lord, help me to forgive." Just then her hand raised and touched his. Then an amazing thing happened. Corrie felt a current run through her shoulder down her arm, enter her hand, and pass to him. At the same time her heart filled with a love for the former soldier.

Later Corrie said that it was that day she discovered that "it is not on our forgiveness any more than on our goodness that the world's healing hinges, but on God's. When he tells us to love our enemies, he gives, along with the command, the love itself."

What Should You Do?

What are some of the things people do to you that really get under your skin?

Is there anyone you have a grudge against now? Can you prayerfully forgive that person even if he or she hasn't asked for forgiveness?

Jeff Frankenstein

"Breathe" was one of the last songs written for our *Take Me To Your Leader* CD. The strange thing that happened was that we were running so far over schedule on recording that we weren't finished by the time a tour came rolling around. We weren't going to cancel dates, so we had to schedule studio time on the road. Some of the studios we ended up in were tucked away in these little towns we were passing through. It was a little weird, not to mention hectic.

Tours are no picnic on your body. Doing the concerts at night, sleeping on the bus, then recording all day started to take a toll on us. Most of us were just getting grouchy, but Peter actually got sick. That's saying something because Peter's one of the strongest dudes I know. We started noticing that the fatigue was even caus-

Tuesday the third, I'll call this entry "Mistake"
Cheap imitation ... my life feels like a fake
A people person ... some days people annoy me
I'm growing edgy
Wednesday's title: "Avoid me"
Breathe on me ... breathe oh Breath of God
Breathe on me till my heart is new
Breathe on me ... breathe oh Breath of Life
Breathe on me till I love like You do
Thursday, the fifth, I title "Drivers Beware"
Tempered-a-mental and I don't really care
I gave till I bled
You laughed when I fainted
Don't want to live this life bitter and tainted

"Breathe"
Newsboys

ing us to be rude to people. And that's the last thing you want to do when you're out there on the road to minister. Honestly, we were just burnt out.

When it finally got to the point that we couldn't go on, we held a band meeting on the bus. Somebody said, "Guys, we just need to stop right here and pray for God to refresh our hearts." We did, and it was wonderful. God really answered our prayers. It was as if he just reached down out of heaven and picked up that huge rock that we were carrying.

Looking back, I think every band member would say that the we went through our own mini-revival that day. In just a few short weeks Peter was back in good health and things got a little more back to normal (if you can call our lives normal). We got a great song out of the experience, and I think it taught us all a good lesson. I don't expect our lives to slow down much, but I'm sure we will be quicker to avail ourselves of God's strength to get us through in the future.

What Would Jesus Do?

One of those days Jesus went out to a mountainside to pray, and spent the night praying to God. (Luke 6:12)

After he had dismissed them, he went up on a mountainside by himself to pray. When evening came, he was there alone. (Matthew 14:23)

They went to a place called Gethsemane, and Jesus said to his disciples, "Sit here while I pray." (Mark 14:32)

About eight days after Jesus said this, he took Peter, John and James with him and went up onto a mountain to pray. (Luke 9:28)

When he rose from prayer and went back to the disciples, he found them asleep, exhausted from sorrow. "Why are you sleeping?" he asked them. "Get up and pray so that you will not fall into temptation." (Luke 22:45–46)

After leaving them, he went up on a mountainside to pray. (Mark 6:46)

The Point!

What is the scariest movie you've ever seen? For me it's a toss-up between *Aliens* and *Jaws*. What struck me about both of these movies is that you knew there was something sinister out there, but you didn't know how bad it was until it was too late. I have the same kind of feeling when I read Ephesians 6. Paul warns us that you may think your greatest enemies out there are the murderers, rapists, and psychopaths, but just like in the movies, it's much worse than you thought. Our battle is with "... authorities, against the powers of this dark world and against the spiritual forces of evil in the heavenly realms" (Ephesians 6:12).

Don't panic. God has given us everything we need to keep us from becoming breakfast for our enemies, as well as to insure that we will win the battle. All we've got to do is use the weapons he has given us. Paul tells us that we've got resources like the belt of truth, the helmet of salvation, the sword of the Spirit—and the list goes on. And finally Paul tells us to do what the disciples saw Jesus do so often—"always pray."

Don't just pray when you hear the *Jaws* music playing in the background of your life. Pray always. Don't allow prayer to become your last resort. Make it your first resource.

Have you burned out from fighting a relentless spiritual battle? Are you just plain beat from wrestling with the "aliens" in your life? Jesus said, "Come to me, all you who are weary and burdened, and I will give you rest" (Matthew 11:28). But you can't get that rest if you can't find time to come to him.

What Should You Do?

What's your private prayer life like? Do you have a regular time to pray each day? If not, what time might be a good time each day to set aside for prayer?

Who among your friends might be willing to pray with you regularly?

Think about a time when you felt "burned out." What could you have prayed that might have helped the situation?

Serene Campbell

You can't do anything, anytime, anywhere
Without thinking about it
There's consequences, consequences
Choices are easily made,
    sometimes hard to erase
That's the price we pay for living
Everything's dark when your eyes are closed
Left or right fork in the road
Play with a bomb and it's going to explode
Deeds are dominoes
Decisions seem like a bore,
    but they're harder to ignore
Deciding what you're living for
Throttle the moment but the moment dies
Make your own truth but it's all a lie
Try to speed up and find that life
    will pass you by
Up or down, fast or slow
All I know is that the boomerang
    will circle round
Back to the hand where it was thrown

"Consequences"
Considering Lily

I can relate to some of the difficult decisions young people are having to make today. I just turned twenty, and I know the pressures that are out there in regard to drugs, alcohol, and premarital sex. The fact that I've successfully kept from giving in to those types of temptations is a credit not so much to me but to the many things God has put in my life to give me strength to do the right thing.

One of my biggest blessings is my family. I come from a large family, and I'm the youngest of six. When you're the youngest in a large

Christian family you have no shortage of people willing to give you spiritual guidance. That may sound like a negative, but it's not. My family has been a protective hedge for me, especially during my high school years.

You may not have a family who gives you a lot of spiritual support, but you can find yourself a support system that can help you stay strong. A church is a good place to look. Ideally, a good support system is made up of people your age and people who are older and wiser—Christians who care about you, who care about Jesus, and who care about staying strong and pure themselves.

I think that many kids are making poor choices because they surround themselves with the wrong people. The Bible says "bad company corrupts good character" (1 Corinthians 15:33). That is certainly true, but I think you could also say "good company builds good character." You can gain a lot of encouragement from seeing a friend reading a Bible instead of a trashy magazine. Or from going to church instead of to a night club. I've had role models like that around me and that's what I want to be for others in Considering Lily.

Another reason I think young people are making so many poor choices is because they don't seem to realize the long-term consequences of some decisions they make every day. Certain decisions may seem small now, but the impact on their hearts may be eternal. If they could just look into the future and see how those choices affect their lives later on, I don't think they would be so willing to go along with the crowd.

There are many people who think they will start standing for Jesus when they get a little older and are more settled. I don't buy this concept of serving God when it's convenient. The longer they wait, the harder it gets, and many will never stand up at all. By the time they get around to it, a thousand seemingly tiny choices will have taken them so far off course that they will never be able to find their way back.

What Did Abraham Do?

The Lord had said to Abram, "Leave your country, your people and your father's household and go to the land I will show you."

So Abram went up from Egypt to the Negev, with his wife and everything he had, and Lot went with him.

Now Lot, who was moving about with Abram, also had flocks and herds and tents. But the land could not support them while they stayed together, for their possessions were so great that they were not able to stay together. And quarreling arose between Abram's herdsmen and the herdsmen of Lot.

So Abram said to Lot, "Let's not have any quarreling between you and me, or between your herdsmen and mine, for we are brothers. Is not the whole land before you? Let's part company. If you go to the left, I'll go to the right; if you go to the right, I'll go to the left."

Lot looked up and saw that the whole plain of the Jordan was well watered, like the garden of the Lord, like the land of Egypt, toward Zoar. (This was before the Lord destroyed Sodom and Gomorrah.) So Lot chose for himself the whole plain of the Jordan and set out toward the east. The two men parted company: Abram lived in the land of Canaan, while Lot lived among the cities of the plain and pitched his tents near Sodom. (Genesis 12:1, 4; 2: 5-12)

The Point!

Abraham's name is found listed in the book of Hebrews' hall of fame of faith (chapter 11) because of his unquestioning obedience to God. God said "get up and go," and by faith Abram got up and went. In fact, after he did so, God rewarded Abram's faithful obedience by promising that he would be the father of many nations. He even changed Abram's name from "Abram" to "Abraham," which means "father of many."

Lot ended up in the hall of fame of faith but some would say, "just barely." His life didn't end up exactly how he planned. He went from being a wealthy herdsman to being a homeless drunk. But it didn't happen overnight. It happened over a lifetime, and all as a result of a series of seemingly small choices.

In spite of the well-known wickedness of the Sodomites, Lot chose to live near their city. He may have rationalized that he wouldn't be infected by them because he was not moving into Sodom, only near it. He may even have said, "Our presence will bring light to a dark place."

We are not given the details, but before you know it Lot *has* moved into Sodom. And a few chapters beyond that, Lot appears to have become a city official. By the time the three angels come to warn Lot that the city is about to be vaporized, his family is deep into sin and his wife is reluctant to leave the city behind. When we last see Lot, his wealth is gone, his wife is a pillar of salt, and he is a homeless drunk.

Small choices can seem as easy to escape from as handcuffs of thread. If I wrap some thread around your arms once or even twice, you can easily break free. But if I continue to circle your wrists they eventually become bound as if by chains of steel.

What Should You Do?

Which of your friends really encourage you to live for Jesus? How do they do this?

How do the CDs you listen to make you feel? In what ways do they help you want to live for God?

What is one thing you are doing that you know is wrong, but hasn't seemed like a big deal? Where might this choice be leading you?

Steve Wiggins

The most difficult moral choice I've had to make in the past three years was to leave my family behind to share Christ with others. And since my son, Wyatt, came along it's been harder than ever. It's very, very difficult to get on that tour bus and wave good-bye to everyone I love most. I believe that my ministry to my own family comes first. Yet, my wife, Misty, and I sat down a few years ago and agreed that the Big Tent Revival ministry was God's will for now. We both agree, and we both have to make sacrifices to do it.

While that decision had clarity a few years ago, it's getting harder to keep that clarity every day. Back

Somethin' 'bout Jesus that makes me forget
All of the silly little cares of this world
Oh yea! You bet! Got into Memphis about 2 a.m.
Waiting for me was my blond-haired friend
Trying to ease my mind
I ain't been home in a long, long time
Start complaining about balancing books
She gives me one of those looks and says
Baby don't get uptight, Jesus gonna make it right
Shine, shine like the star of Bethlehem
Shine, shine on the one who died and rose again
Some men, they worry about family
Some even worry about time for tea
But there's one man I'll say
Who can chase those worries away
His name is Jesus and soon you will know
Shout His name and watch your worries go
Trust in Jesus Christ, He died to give you life

"Something Bout Jesus"
Big Tent Revival

then, I was able to look Misty in the eye and say, "I believe this is God's will for me," and she looked right back and said, "I agree, go for it." But I can't do that with Wyatt. If I were to ask him, "Son, do you think I ought to get on the bus with Spence and go tell people about Jesus or do you want Daddy to stay home?" I know which one he would pick. And the problem is going to get worse soon because Misty and I are going to have a baby girl.

I remember back in the Old Testament how Eli was a holy man of God and a prophet, yet his sons grew up to be worthless. I don't want to save other people's kids and lose my own. I don't want my kids growing up saying, "There goes Dad again, putting on his Jesus hat to go out and sell a few T-shirts." I've got to make sure that I don't neglect my own family. When I'm home, I need to live in such a way that I show them that Jesus is first, they are second, and Big Tent Revival comes after that.

By far the most difficult moral choice I have ever had to make happens every day for me now: simply being on the road and not at home with my family. It's a balancing act that can only be pulled off successfully by being sensitive to God's will and not my own.

What Would Jesus Do?

On the third day a wedding took place at Cana in Galilee. Jesus' mother was there, and Jesus and his disciples had also been invited to the wedding. When the wine was gone, Jesus' mother said to him, "They have no more wine."

"Dear woman, why do you involve me?" Jesus replied. "My time has not yet come." His mother said to the servants, "Do whatever he tells you."

Nearby stood six stone water jars, the kind used by the Jews for ceremonial washing, each holding from twenty to thirty gallons. Jesus said to the servants, "Fill the jars with water"; so they filled them to the brim.

Then he told them, "Now draw some out and take it to the master of the banquet." They did so, and the master of the banquet tasted the water that had been turned into wine. He did not realize where it had come from, though the servants who had drawn the water knew. Then he called the bridegroom aside and said, "Everyone brings out the choice wine first and then the cheaper wine after the guests have had too much to drink; but you have saved the best till now."

This, the first of his miraculous signs, Jesus performed at Cana in Galilee. He thus revealed his glory, and his disciples put their faith in him. (John 2:1–11)

The Point!

The record of Jesus' first miracle is so controversial that often the most important message is lost. Some focus on the wine issue. Others think Jesus was being disrespectful to his mother, when in fact the opposite is true. To get the real picture of what happened at this wedding party, maybe you need to hear what Paul Harvey calls "the rest of the story."

Jesus grew up in a big family, at least by today's standard. He had four brothers and at least two sisters (Mark 6:3). Most scholars believe that sometime between Jesus' visit to Jerusalem at age twelve and the launch of his ministry at thirty, his father, Joseph, must have died. The Bible mentions Mary and the rest of the family many more times, but Joseph seems to have disappeared. Mary is even an eye witness of the crucifixion, but where's Joseph?

If Joseph was indeed dead, this explains why Jesus waited until he was thirty years old to begin his life's calling. In Jesus' day the eldest son took over responsibility for providing for the family in the event of the father's death. He had an obligation that continued until the children were grown or his mother released him from his duty.

So, let's take another look at that wedding scene. Mary sees a friend about to be embarrassed because the refreshments are running out. She knows Jesus can solve the problem. He's probably already walked on water in the bathtub or something. She knows Jesus won't act unless she releases him from his family duties. If he turns that water to wine, there is no way he can go back to being the humble village carpenter. The genie will be out of the bottle, so to speak, and there will be no going back.

Can you imagine, here is God incarnate, the Messiah who has come to save the world, saying, "Okay, Mom, is this it? Has my time come to put down my hammer and pick up a cross?" Only Mary could answer that question, because it was up to her. And Mary, flush with feelings that only a mother losing a son can understand says, "Yes, save the party, then go save the world."

This story is not about wine or even miracles. It's about a faithful son who realized that ministry starts with your own family first. Jesus was first a good son and then became the Savior of humanity.

 # What Should You Do?

How's your relationship with your family—mom, dad, brothers, sisters? What would it take to make those relationships better?

In the way you handle your responsibilities, how are you letting your family see Jesus in you?

Ken Steorts

"Whirlwind" is kind of an unusual way of looking at the advancing plan of God. It's about his will and his irresistible

> Talking to God, hearing what he wants
> He moves in violence, I stand in silence
> Who can question you, who can fathom you?
> In your presence, who can stand?
> Worlds spin around and kings crumble down
> There's no escaping what you've planned
> Winds approaching, clouds are forming
> God in his power is swirling around me
> Calling me—and you know my name
> It's alright, it's alright
> Jump in the whirlwind
> I'm letting go
> My world's at stake, I want to break
> Stop the striving, start the dying
> There's no arguing what you say
> Master and Savior, Sustainer and Creator
> You move in power, winds and thunder
> I'm letting go
>
> "Whirlwind"
> Skillet

power, and how you can either cooperate with his plan or you can resist it and be swept away. From the song's point of view, being in the whirlwind of God is the safest place you could be. It can be awesome, even terrifying, but the best place for a believer to be is caught up into his power and might.

A few years ago, I was going through a very difficult time in my life. I was really struggling, and when I'm struggling sometimes my first instinct is to bail out. I've always wanted to live up in the Northwest. I love the mountains. In fact, the guys in the band call me "nature boy." I guess I'm just a late-blooming hippie. Anyway, when tough times found me in Memphis, I thought it was time I should be traveling on.

I'm no stranger to moving around. My dad was in the Air Force. He was constantly transferred, so I grew up moving a lot. There's kind of a safety about moving; you just pick up and start all over. There's no past to worry about. Everything is new.

Well, about the time I was looking to start fresh someplace else, God providentially led me to a guy named Rick Miller. Rick cared for me, discipled me, and stood by me with what some people would call "tough love." One of the things he encouraged me to do was face my storm head on. For me, that meant staying in the church and staying in Memphis.

It was not the most comfortable thing to do. For a while it felt just like I was jumping into the whirlwind, but I'm so thankful I did. I met the guys in Skillet, I found my wife, Joy, and most importantly, no matter how hard the winds blew, I knew there would always be peace and safety in the center of God's will.

What Did Jesus Do?

Now at the Feast the Jews were watching for him and asking, "Where is that man?"

Among the crowds there was widespread whispering about him. Some said, "He is a good man."

Others replied, "No, he deceives the people." But no one would say anything publicly about him for fear of the Jews.

Not until halfway through the Feast did Jesus go up to the temple courts and begin to teach. The Jews were amazed and asked, "How did this man get such learning without having studied?"

Jesus answered, "My teaching is not my own. It comes from him who sent me. If anyone chooses to do God's will, he will find out whether my teaching comes from God or whether I speak on my own...."

At that point some of the people of Jerusalem began to ask, "Isn't this the man they are trying to kill? Here he is, speaking publicly, and they are not saying a word to him. Have the authorities really concluded that he is the Christ? But we know where this man is from; when the Christ comes, no one will know where he is from." Then Jesus, still teaching in the temple courts, cried out, "Yes, you know me, and you know where I am from. I am not here on my own, but he who sent me is true. You do not know him, but I know him because I am from him and he sent me." At this they tried to seize him, but no one laid a hand on him, because his time had not yet come. Still, many in the crowd put their faith in him. They said, "When the Christ comes, will he do more miraculous signs than this man?" (John 7:11–17, 25–31)

The Point!

Being in the center of God's will is something like being in the eye of a hurricane. As the fearful storm approaches the swirling outer winds can hit at speeds of up to two hundred miles an hour. As it hits the shore, the winds rage and howl, uprooting trees, hurling cars, and leveling houses. It may blow steadily for an hour or more and then suddenly the wind just stops. The sun peaks through and the birds start to sing. Has the storm ended? Far from it. You've simply moved into a twenty-mile wide region at the center of the hurricane where things are so peaceful that—if it were not for the incredible damage all around you—it would be hard to believe any storm existed at all.

In the center of God's will is always peace and safety. The winds may blow around you and the lightening may explode, but in the heart of his plan there is calm. The only thing you ever need to fear is venturing outside of it.

What Should You Do?

What things in your past are you least proud of—or most hurt by?

What obstacles in your life are keeping you from total surrender to God's will?

What might he ask you to be, go, or give up, that scares you? What can you find in his character than can help you trust his will is for your good?

Michael Tait

A few weeks ago, I went with four of my friends to the Smokey Mountains to do some rock climbing. We came to this little town, kind of in the sticks, just outside of Knoxville. I wanted to pull over and get something to drink and I saw a little country store ahead. The ironic thing was that, just as we pulled up I said, "Guys, no telling what they might do to a black man around here." I was just kidding. Even though I've felt subtle prejudice in my day, thank God I've never had to live with the kind of racism that was common a generation ago. All the guys laughed, slapped me on the back, and said, "Don't worry, Mike, we white guys will take care of you."

Well, I walked in and there were three guys sitting there giving me looks I have never seen before. The older of the three said, "You don't belong around here—boy."

At first I thought, "Is he talking to me?" Then I realized he

"We've got some difficult days ahead. But it really doesn't matter with me now. Because I've been to the mountain top. I won't mind. Like anybody, I would like to live a long life. Longevity has its place. But I'm not concerned about that now. I just want to do God's will. And He's allowed me to go up to the mountain. And I've looked over and I've seen the Promised Land. I may not get there with you, but I want you to know tonight that we as a people will get to the Promised Land. So I'm happy tonight. I'm not worried about anything. I'm not fearing any man. Mine eyes have seen the glory of the coming of the Lord."

*Martin Luther King Jr.,
just before his assassination*

98

was. I knew my dreds made me look different than the locals, but hair style wasn't what this was about. He was talking about the color of my skin. I couldn't believe my ears when he said, "You stick around here after dark and we'll hang you." I was thinking, "Man, we're sending rockets to Mars and there are still people living in this kind of blind ignorance." It was as if I had been beamed back to the fifties. Suddenly I was experiencing hatred, the kind of bigotry that I had only read about or seen on TV. I will never forget how I felt in that little country store. For just a split second I felt less than human. I felt alone.

No, I didn't lose it. I just calmly and articulately explained to him that racism is a thing of America's past. I was even surprised myself at the restraint I showed. I knew Jesus would not have lashed out. And to tell you the truth, I think my calm made that man madder than anything else I could have said or done.

I'm okay now, but for the next hour of the drive I didn't want to talk about it.

If any good came from the whole experience it was that I found a deeper respect for those of my race who struggled for civil rights. I also answered some questions about myself. I've always wondered how I might respond to prejudice aimed directly at me. Now I know.

What Would Jesus Do?

So he came to a town in Samaria called Sychar, near the plot of ground Jacob had given to his son Joseph. Jacob's well was there, and Jesus, tired as he was from the journey, sat down by the well. It was about the sixth hour.

When a Samaritan woman came to draw water, Jesus said to her, "Will you give me a drink?" (His disciples had gone into the town to buy food.)

The Samaritan woman said to him, "You are a Jew and I am a Samaritan woman. How can you ask me for a drink?" (For Jews do not associate with Samaritans.)

Jesus answered her, "If you knew the gift of God and who it is that asks you for a drink, you would have asked him and he would have given you living water." ... The woman said to him, "Sir, give me this water so that I won't get thirsty and have to keep coming here to draw water." (John 4:5–10, 15)

The Point!

To get the full impact of this story of Jesus and the woman at the well, I have to explain a couple of things about Bible translation. Have you ever used the expression, "That's Greek to me"? Well, unless you're a language scholar, you probably meant, "I don't understand." Not many folks speak ancient Greek, which is what most of the New Testament was originally written in. That's precisely why the Bible was translated into modern English. That's the good part. The bad part is that some things get lost in the translation, and here's an example.

In this story we read, "Jews do not associate with Samaritans," but quite literally what the original language says is, "They don't share dishes with them." So you see, it's not just that Jesus was willing to "associate" with this Samaritan women, he was even willing to drink after she did. Now, that's not quite the same as asking to borrow someone's toothbrush, but it's still getting up close and personal!

You see, the Samaritans were originally from the Jewish tribe of Ephraim, but they intermarried with so-called "pagan foreigners." So the Jews regarded them as half-breeds and treated them much like pre-civil rights blacks were treated in the fifties and sixties.

That's what blew away the Samaritan woman. She expected to be insulted or at least ignored by Jewish people. She had been treated by them as subhuman her whole life. Yet this Jew did not look on her with the hatred and bigotry to which she was accustomed. Instead, he was kind and humble. He even went so low as to ask her for a favor. And, in the end, he extended to her love and compassion. Jesus looked beyond the woman's gender, race, color, and even her promiscuous past and saw only a human being in deep need of forgiveness.

Go and do what Jesus did!

What Should You Do?

Have you ever felt uncomfortable around people of another race? Why?

Why do you think racism still survives? What fuels it?

What about other kinds of prejudices—against people who are richer or poorer than you, people who dress really different, or people who are in some other way very different from you? Do you tend to think of these people as less than you?

Pete Stewart

I wrote the words to "Fuse" the day after the Olympic Park bombing. I was riding in the van after a show, thinking about what kind of maniac would set off a bomb with the intention of killing innocent people. The Olympics are supposed to be a celebration of how civilized nations can come together in peace. In the midst of this supposed peace a lunatic decides to murder a bunch of people while they watch a concert in a park. And I'm guessing he was thinking he had made some kind of twisted point.

"Fuse" is not just about our present messed-up world, it's about the sin of mankind both past and present. People killed Jesus nearly two thousand years ago, but it would be a mistake to believe it wouldn't happen to day. The remarkable thing to me is not that people were evil two thousand years ago; we've been mur-

Take a look around you,
*   can't you feel the disease*
Some want to save their soul,
*   some save the trees*
The whole world is going down
Like a bottle rocket flies to its death
And I can't help but think
That I might barely make it
*   to my last breath*
How long can someplace last
*   that's dominated by*
F–15s, M–16s, grenades and 45s?
People hate and can't relate
*   to ourselves*
The smell of hell is growing well
Escape from what I deserve is
*   something I would never sell*
Does anybody else see this as irony?
We strive to live for peace
And we nailed Him to our tree

"Fuse"
grammatrain

dering each other since Cain killed Abel. The remarkable thing is that we are still doing it.

I think that to believe human beings are getting better and more civilized is a myth. Sure, we are gaining in technology, but that same science is often used to make more efficient tools with which to kill people. We are growing in knowledge, but the newspaper proves pretty convincingly that we are not growing in wisdom or morality.

To me, humankind's lack of moral growth is one of the strongest reasons to believe every word Jesus said. Jesus made it very clear that knowledge is not a cure for our sinful condition. Science isn't the cure either, because ignorance isn't the sickness. The problem with people is sin, and Jesus is the only one who can fix that.

What Would Jesus Do?

Now while he was in Jerusalem at the Passover Feast, many people saw the miraculous signs he was doing and believed in his name. But Jesus would not entrust himself to them, for he knew all men. He did not need man's testimony about man, for he knew what was in a man. (John 2:23–25)

The Point!

It sometimes amazes me what good, intelligent people will believe. Some folks just don't want to be confused by the facts. My grandmother, for instance, went to her grave believing the moon landing was a hoax. On my list with her, I would also include people who believe in wrestling on TV, evolution, and that Elvis is alive. In the same category I would also put those among us who cling to what I call "the myth of moral evolution." This is the notion that through education, social programs, and self-determination, humans can and will become less sinful.

The problem with the theory of moral evolution is that it rests on some false assumptions. It assumes that people are bad because they are poor, uneducated, or lack nurturing encouragement and moral support. Yet this is not at all what Jesus believed. He taught that sin was less a matter of circumstance and more a matter of birth. Jesus wasn't surprised when people around him sinned. The Scripture both predicts and explains our love affair with sin. It says people sin because that is their nature.

It's like the scorpion who asked the turtle to give him a ride on the turtle's back across the river. The turtle agreed but said, "First you must promise not to sting me." And the scorpion promised with all his heart that he would not. Just as they reached the river's halfway mark, the turtle felt a painful sting on his neck. He turned in astonishment and said, "Why did you do that? Don't you know that now you will drown?" And the scorpion said, "I had to sting you; I'm a scorpion and that's what scorpions do."

People sin because we have to. We are born with a sinful nature and when we act naturally, that is how we behave. Jesus knew this very well. And he also knew that our sinful nature is a birth defect that can never be repaired by government, school, family, or even the church. You see, our inherited sinful nature cannot be repaired or reformed. It must be crucified daily on Christ's cross so that it might ultimately be totally replaced with a brand new one.

What Should You Do?

What are some of the attitudes or actions in your life that are a result of your new nature in Christ?

What are some of your attitudes or actions that remind you that your old sinful nature isn't quite dead yet?

Who normally wins when your old nature and new nature wrestle for the steering wheel of your life?

Bob Herdman

Looking back, I'd be safe in saying that I grew up in one of the most religious families in Ohio. I was saved at age nine and went to church every Sunday morning, every Sunday night, and even attended every revival service that came along. After high school I was looking to get away from all that and take a look at the wild side of life for a change. I joined the Army and soon found myself training with the Rangers. In just a few short months my life was way different from what it was in the sleepy Ohio town where I grew up. I was jumping out of airplanes, going through diving school, and marching through forests in the middle of the night.

And of course I was hanging out with guys who never gave a passing thought to serving God. In fact, just the opposite was true. I won't go into too many details, but we spent a lot of our free time trying to live up to our reputation as one of America's most hard-fighting and hard-partying elite units.

Over the next four years, I got really close to three of the guys. Some of the stuff we had to do together really created a strong bond. You'd think that this might have been a real chance for me to be a light in a dark place, but I kept my light pretty well unplugged. I got so caught up

> You are the light of the world. A city on a hill cannot be hidden. Neither do people light a lamp and put it under a bowl. Instead they put it on its stand, and it gives light to everyone in the house. In the same way, let your light shine before men, that they may see your good deeds and praise your Father in heaven.
>
> Matthew 5:14–16

in living out the Ranger's macho thing that I never got the courage to share Christ with my pals. It's kind of ironic that I was training to risk my life for my country but I was afraid to risk my reputation for Jesus. I knew in my heart I was being a pansy, and sometimes it really bugged me. I remember I was out with the guys and we saw someone bow to pray before they ate. One of my Ranger friends started to make fun of him. It really made me mad, but not mad enough to stand up for my faith.

When I got out of the Rangers, God really started dealing with me. I felt terribly guilty about never sharing the gospel with my friends. I prayed for them every day, yet felt that a chance to make a difference in their lives was lost forever. Then one day, just after a concert in Tacoma, here came Michael Lee, one of my Ranger buddies. To my amazement, he was talking about God! He had given his life to Christ, and to top it off, I found out that one of my other friends had made the decision to trust Jesus, too.

I can't tell you what great news that was. I may have been too afraid to share my faith, but thank God, someone else wasn't. That's two down and one to go, but instead of it being one praying for three, now there's three praying for one.

What Did Peter Do?

The priests and the captain of the temple guard and the Sadducees came up to Peter and John while they were speaking to the people. They were greatly disturbed because the apostles were teaching the people and proclaiming in Jesus the resurrection of the dead. They seized Peter and John, and because it was evening, they put them in jail until the next day. But many who heard the message believed, and the number of men grew to about five thousand.

Then they called them in again and commanded them not to speak or teach at all in the name of Jesus. But Peter and John replied, "Judge for yourselves whether it is right in God's sight to obey you rather than God. For we cannot help speaking about what we have seen and heard." (Acts 4:1–4,18–20)

The Point!

One of the most difficult questions people ask throughout their lives is, "Where do I fit in?" Like the chameleon, we feel most comfortable when we are convinced that we blend in seamlessly with our surroundings. For the chameleon, the need for camouflage is a real means of protection from hungry predators. Better to look like the surrounding rocks than to end up on the wrong end of a dinner date!

It's probably a similar fear that makes humans like to feel invisible in the crowd. No, not that we fear becoming anyone's "Mac-lunch" literally, but we all hold real fears of being wounded emotionally. Rejection, humiliation, or just plain old being laughed at can virtually eat a person alive. Fear of rejection can also persuade us to be silent about some of our most strongly embraced beliefs.

Jesus was constantly called a liar, a demon, and a traitor by his own people. He was eventually betrayed by one of his twelve closest disciples and abandoned by the other eleven. Finally, he was nailed to a cross naked, complete with a sarcastic head board that read "King of the Jews."

Jesus knew all this pain could have been averted by simply making a few adjustments to his message and slipping safely and comfortably into the religious environment of the day. He could have easily avoided a splintered cross by becoming a part of the spiritual woodwork.

So why would Jesus choose the cross? I guess no one had advised him of the ancient proverb, "it's better to be a living dog than a dead lion." Or perhaps it was because Jesus believed that pleasing God was something more valuable than the crowd's acceptance—even more precious than life itself.

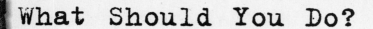

What Should You Do?

What is the worst thing you could lose by telling your friends about your faith in Christ?

When would be the best time to shoot straight with your friends about your beliefs? How do you think each of them will react?

Is it possible that some of your friends may already share your belief in God but are afraid to talk about it? Which ones?

How will you feel if your friends never come to know Jesus as Savior?

Michael Johnston

Being in Christian music has taught me to live on very little. I know it doesn't look like it to a public that just sees us on stage, but we've been through some pretty rough times. I guess until recently you could have classified me as homeless. I've had to learn to trust God each day to provide for just my basic needs. In many ways that's been a good thing because it's taught me how little a person really needs to be happy.

It hasn't always been that way for me. I worked all through high school. I drove a tractor on my uncle's tobacco farm, I was gardener for a while, a grocery store courtesy clerk (okay, a bag boy), and I drove a delivery truck for a construction supply company. So in high school, I got used to having a little money in my pockets.

I remember my big dream was to save up for a Jeep. It seems like a small thing now, but it was huge for me then.

Yesterday I lived for me
And I was so alone as I could be
Then I saw you and how you
* give yourself away*
And I want to live for you today
I'll give; I'll hold nothing
I'll give and I'll hold nothing back
My love is a lot like me
Wanting nothing less than everything
But I know you're the only love that's true
And only giving makes me close to you
My hands are open, so take what you see
And I'll keep nothing, hold nothing
* back from me*

"I'll Give"
Smalltown Poets

When God called me into Christian music, I knew I had to choose between two lifestyles. I didn't go into this ministry with my eyes closed. I knew that it might be a long time before I'd see that Jeep, maybe never. Until recently, I was pretty convinced it would the latter.

Just when I started to get kind of comfortable with my apparent destiny to be poor, one of our records became a hit. I sat up the other night on the bus wondering what success was going to feel like, and more importantly, was it going to change me? I started thinking about the Sermon on the Mount and Jesus saying, "Where your treasure is, there your heart will be also" (Matthew 6:21). I thought back on how miserably poor I've been up until now, and yet I've been really happy. God has been so faithful.

I made up my mind that the most important thing for me is to be at peace in my relationship with God. I won't allow money or fame to steal that from me. No matter what battle I've got to fight, no matter what I have to give up, peace with God has always got to be what guides my decisions in life.

What Did Jesus Do?

Now when he saw the crowds, he went up on a mountainside and sat down. His disciples came to him, and he began to teach them, saying: "(Do not store up for yourselves treasures on earth, where moth and rust destroy, and where thieves break in and steal. But store up for yourselves treasures in heaven, where moth and rust do not destroy, and where thieves do not break in and steal. For where your treasure is, there your heart will be also.... You cannot serve both God and Money.)"

"Therefore I tell you, do not worry about your life, what you will eat or drink; or about your body, what you will wear. Is not life more important than food, and the body more important than clothes? And why do you worry about clothes? See how the lilies of the field grow. They do not labor or spin. Yet I tell you that not even Solomon in all his splendor was dressed like one of these. If that is how God clothes the grass of the field, which is here today and tomorrow is thrown into the fire, will he not much more clothe you, O you of little faith?

"So do not worry, saying, 'What shall we eat?' or 'What shall we drink?' or 'What shall we wear?' For the pagans run after all these things, and your heavenly Father knows that you need them. But seek first his kingdom and his righteousness, and all these things will be given to you as well. Therefore do not worry about tomorrow, for tomorrow will worry about itself. Each day has enough trouble of its own." (Matthew 5:1,2, 6:19–21, 24b–34)

The Point!

God doesn't have a problem with our having possessions. He has a problem with our possessions possessing us. If you own things, that's great. If things own you, you're in big trouble. You see, God wants you to trust him every day for what you need. He has promised that if you will live for him, he will prove to you that he is a loving Father by taking care of you as his own child. God's integrity is on the line here, but he can't prove his faithfulness to you if you are unwilling to trust him.

No matter how much clutter you cram into your life, none of it has lasting value. Jim Elliot once said, "He is no fool who gives what he cannot keep to gain what he cannot lose." As a missionary, Jim had already given a lot to God. Months later, Jim was called on to give what none of us can keep—he gave his life on the mission field. The point is this, the only thing we have that death can't kill, thieves can't steal, and rust can't destroy is Jesus. A wise person will keep his treasure safe in him.

What Should You Do?

List some of the things you really want—anything at all.

Identify those things on the list that are eternal.

Which of the things on your list do you really need in order to live peacefully and happily?

Ben Cissell

The path that brought me to Audio Adrenaline was pretty bizarre. I became a Christian at a Young Life camp and before you know it, my life turned schizophrenic. I remember one weekend I was playing with my jazz combo in a competition on Saturday afternoon, that night I played in a bar band, and on Sunday morning I played in the praise and worship band at my church. With each band I was surrounded by totally different kinds of people. Maybe that's one of the reasons I just up and decided to leave St. Louis and move down to Nashville.

I dropped out of college, left my bands, and moved in with a friend who was playing with East to West. I was there only two weeks when I ran into Audio Adrenaline's manager, who gave me a job selling T-shirts for the band. It must have sounded weird to my parents when I called home and told them I had left college and my own bands to be a roadie for someone else. I didn't know why, but deep inside I knew it was the right thing to do.

Some musicians might have thought it was beneath them to sell T-shirts and run errands, but I didn't. I didn't know

> *Jesus ... got up from the meal, took off his outer clothing, and wrapped a towel around his waist. After that, he poured water into a basin and began to wash his disciples' feet, drying them with the towel that was wrapped around him. "Now that I, your Lord and Teacher, have washed your feet, you also should wash one another's feet. I have set you an example that you should do as I have done for you."*
>
> *John 13:3–5, 14–15*

very much about Christian music and this was giving me time to learn. It was kind of a wilderness experience for me, and I'm thankful I didn't have to stay there long. After six months, I got the chance to audition with band and got the job.

What Would Jesus Do?

If you have any encouragement from being united with Christ, if any comfort from his love, if any fellowship with the Spirit, if any tenderness and compassion, then make my joy complete by being like-minded, having the same love, being one in spirit and purpose. Do nothing out of selfish ambition or vain conceit, but in humility consider others better than yourselves. Each of you should look not only to your own interests, but also to the interests of others. Your attitude should be the same as that of Christ Jesus: Who, being in very nature God, did not consider equality with God something to be grasped, but made himself nothing, taking the very nature of a servant, being made in human likeness. And being found in appearance as a man, he humbled himself and became obedient to death—even death on a cross!

Therefore God exalted him to the highest place and gave him the name that is above every name, that at the name of Jesus every knee should bow, in heaven and on earth and under the earth, and every tongue confess that Jesus Christ is Lord, to the glory of God the Father. (Philippians 2:1–11)

The Point!

There is a great deal of confusion in the church today about the meaning of humility. Everyone knows that Christians should be humble, but few know exactly what that means. Perhaps the best way to discover real humility is to examine what it's not.

First, a humble person is not one who lies about his or her own ability. If you have a talent, gift, or ability, you shouldn't pretend you don't. But do remember where you got the gift and that you must use it in a way that ultimately gives Christ the standing ovation. Your gift wasn't given to make others look small, it was given to make Jesus look big.

Second, humility isn't about thinking negatively about self; it's about not thinking of self at all. We are all created in God's image, and that gives us all incredible value. To try to make yourself think negatively about his creation is an insult to God. God has commanded us to love our neighbors in the same way we love ourselves. If you don't love the you that God made, you won't be able to love your neighbor in the way God intended.

Third, never compare yourself to others; they are not our measuring stick, God is.

Finally, don't waste time seeking humility. Just seek God. As you find him and see him as he is, that will be enough to keep you humble.

What Should You Do?

If you had a class project and you did most of the work, how would you feel if someone else got most of the glory?

What would you do?

What are your strengths and abilities? Where did they come from?

What are some of the ways in which God might have prepared you—by giving you talents and opportunities, for instance—to serve him?

Steve Wiggins

BIG TENT REVIVAL

Sometimes, sitting in an autograph line, there will be a person that you can just tell is there for more than an autograph. They want to connect with you. They've been at home in their room listening to Big Tent Revival and something you said really moved them. Sure, in a perfect world I'd love to give this person all the time they needed, but that's not always possible. There's usually people in line behind him or her growing restless, or an anxious store owner pacing nearby wanting to make sure you get to everybody, or maybe it's as basic as you and the guys know that as soon as the last person passes through the line, you can get some much-needed sleep. Sometimes helping people is just plain inconvenient and you've got to choose between yourself and the person who needs you.

The other night we had just finished a concert at Liberty University. In order to get out to the autograph table without going through the crowd, security escorted me behind some bleachers. Out of the darkness came this guy who had been waiting for me. My first thought was maybe this guy was some nut with a gun. You never know. Anyway, he came up to me and said, "Man, I really connected to what you were saying up there. Can you talk to me for a little while?"

> Then little children were brought to Jesus for him to place his hands on them and pray for them. But the disciples rebuked those who brought them. Jesus said, "Let the little children come to me, and do not hinder them, for the kingdom of heaven belongs to such as these."
>
> Matthew 19:13–14

Meanwhile I had a road manager pulling my arm saying, "Wiggins, we've got to go," and all I could think of was that I was already beat and this could take hours.

Well, to make a long story short, a couple of hours later, I found myself in an empty auditorium, sitting in the bleachers, leading this guy to Jesus. I guess the moral to this story is that people can't always need you when it's convenient, and even if you're singing at a Christian university, don't take anything for granted.

What Would Jesus Do?

One day Jesus said to his disciples, "Let's go over to the other side of the lake." So they got into a boat and set out. As they sailed, he fell asleep. A squall came down on the lake, so that the boat was being swamped, and they were in great danger.

The disciples went and woke him, saying, "Master, Master, we're going to drown!"

He got up and rebuked the wind and the raging waters; the storm subsided, and all was calm. "Where is your faith?" he asked his disciples.

In fear and amazement they asked one another, "Who is this? He commands even the winds and the water, and they obey him." (Luke 8:22–25)

The Point!

After Jesus turned water into wine at the wedding in Cana, the cat was out of the bag. His life was never the same. He went from total obscurity to being a virtual superstar over night. Huge crowds followed him everywhere he went. They came to him constantly, wanting wisdom, healing, forgiveness, miracles, and his blessing. They shouted for him and grasped at his clothing. No wonder that most of his time with his Father seemed to take place in the middle of the night. It was probably the only time he could be alone!

When Jesus had finally found a few minutes to rest on a boat, a storm begins to brew. The disciples were terrified by the intensity of the wind and the waves, but no one wanted to wake Jesus. It was a tough call for the disciples: Either face the wrath of Jesus or the fury of the storm. They opted to take their chances with Jesus.

When Jesus woke up, he did do some serious rebuking. First, he rebuked the wind and the waves and they are silenced. Then he turned to the disciples. No, not for waking him, because you can take a problem to Jesus any time you want. He rebuked them for not showing a little faith.

You see, Jesus knows you can't schedule the storms in your life. He was well aware that the storms of life rarely submit to our schedules. More often, it rains when there isn't an umbrella or storm shelter in sight. Jesus had hoped that his disciples would have learned by now that even if the storms of life catch us when we are least prepared, God is always ready and willing to give us what we need to see us through.

What Should You Do?

Who do you know who could use more of your time?

What project in your community or at church could you become involved in with a little sacrifice on your part?

What kinds of activities could you give up in order to find the time to help someone else?

Rebecca St.James

Speak to me Lord for your child is here listening
Speak to me Lord for your child is here
*   waiting on you*
Unveil my eyes let me see ... see you
Unveil my heart let me know ... know you
Father do
You are the true God
*   the one living Lord ... Father*
You are the true God
*   the one living Lord ... Father you*
Unveil my eyes let me see ... see you
Unveil my heart let know ... know you
Father do
Jesus your word stands forever
Changing me forever
Speak to me Lord for your child is here listening
Speak to me Lord for your child is here
*   waiting on you*
Unveil my eyes let me see ... see you
Unveil my heart let know ... know you
Speak to me Lord for your child is here

"Speak To Me"
Rebecca St. James

I grew up in Sydney, Australia, and because of my dad I was constantly around people involved in contemporary Christian music. My father was one of only a couple of people in our country who organized and promoted CCM concerts. Even though I loved some of the people I met and saw how God was using their music, I never dreamed that God would someday use me in that way.

When I was thirteen, I auditioned for an outreach rock

band at my school. I was a little surprised when I was chosen. One of my teachers also really believed in me and this gave me courage. For the first time, I got affirmation outside my family that God might want to use my voice. When we moved to the States, I continued to sing on and off with my youth group at churches and even in an occasional prison.

You might think that it would just occur to my family that I should grow up and become a music artist. I mean, Dad had all this experience with and connections in Christian music, but that was part of the problem. He didn't want his thirteen-year-old little girl in music full time. Dad had seen the other side of a Christian singer's life. He knew about the financial struggles and the time you must spend away from your family.

The turning point took place during a concert I did at a maximum security prison in Macon, Georgia. My mum and dad were concerned at first because there I was, a fifteen-year-old girl, singing to all these murderers. My dad was worried that we might be taken hostage or something. Yet, it turned out to be one of the most incredible times of worship I have ever experienced. God moved in such an unbelievable way. Those men just poured out their hearts to the Lord. But God was not only moving in the hearts of those prisoners that day; he also spoke very clearly to my father and me: This was the ministry God wanted me to pursue.

What Would Jesus Do?

"I tell you the truth, the man who does not enter the sheep pen by the gate, but climbs in by some other way, is a thief and a robber. The man who enters by the gate is the shepherd of his sheep. The watchman opens the gate for him, and the sheep listen to his voice. He calls his own sheep by name and leads them out. When he has brought out all his own, he goes on ahead of them, and his sheep follow him because they know his voice. But they will never follow a stranger; in fact, they will run away from him because they do not recognize a stranger's voice." Jesus used this figure of speech, but they did not understand what he was telling them.

Therefore Jesus said again, "I tell you the truth, I am the gate for the sheep. All who ever came before me were thieves and robbers, but the sheep did not listen to them. I am the gate; whoever enters through me will be saved. He will come in and go out, and find pasture. The thief comes only to steal and kill and destroy; I have come that they may have life, and have it to the full.

"I am the good shepherd. The good shepherd lays down his life for the sheep. The hired hand is not the shepherd who owns the sheep. So when he sees the wolf coming, he abandons the sheep and runs away. Then the wolf attacks the flock and scatters it. The man runs away because he is a hired hand and cares nothing for the sheep.

"I am the good shepherd; I know my sheep and my sheep know me—just as the Father knows me and I know the Father—and I lay down my life for the sheep." (John 10:1–15)

The Point!

The Bible mentions sheep over 750 times the Bible, and in nearly half of those references the Bible is referring to us, God's people. You may think it's great to be compared to those cuddly fuzz balls, but if you really look at it, the image of a sheep is not entirely flattering. At the risk of being insensitive, sheep are just plain dumb.

In Psalm 23:2 David says, "He leads me beside quiet waters." That's because sheep are afraid of bubbling water. They will die of thirst rather than go near it. Isaiah 53:6 says, "We all, like sheep, have gone astray" and that's because sheep so easily lose their way. Sheep have a tendency to graze while paying no attention to their surroundings. It is not unusual for a lamb to walk right off a cliff munching a mouth full of grass!

The good news is that we have a wonderful Shepherd and we know his voice. In ancient Israel, when a shepherd needed to go into town for supplies he had to pack up the whole flock and march them right into town. The shepherd would enter by a special gate ingeniously called "the sheep gate." Here, in one big pen, all visiting shepherds would leave their flocks.

Perhaps it occurs to you that this might present a problem when it was time to leave because the sheep weren't tagged or even counted. Yet their shepherds had no difficulty leaving with exactly the number they came with. Here's why: Sheep form an incredible bond with their shepherd. They know him and they trust no others. They recognize his voice and are frightened by the sound of strange shepherds. The shepherd needed only to open the gate and call and his sheep alone would follow. All the others would scurry to the back of the pen.

In the same way, sometimes our Shepherd calls for us to move to pastures that are unfamiliar and unexpected. But that's no reason to panic. As long as we are carefully listening and closely following, we will be safe in any field where he leads.

 # What Should You Do?

What are some of the ways God speaks to you? How do you recognize his voice?

When in your life have you felt God was calling you to "move on to new pastures"?

The Last Word!

When I was about seven, my mom would say, "Son, remember, you are what you eat." I thought long and hard about what it would feel like to, in reality, be a pizza and a side order of fries. Later on, I became a Christian and discovered "you are what you think." A better way to say it might be "you act like how you think."

My first day in high school my chemistry teacher, Mr. Adair, told me that I came from a monkey. He didn't mean just me, he meant everyone. And he really seemed happy about it. I was thinking, "If we really came from monkeys, maybe we should be quiet about it. This is no laughing matter."

Later on Mr. Adair told us that when people die they just rot. He said they decompose into about seven dollars and fifty cents worth of mineral deposit as if we were supposed to be excited about the future. In the same semester, he told us that people were just smart animals. We're here on earth to survive by tooth or claw or any means possible.

I wasn't the brightest kid in the world, but after a while I started putting all this together. What I heard my teachers saying is that I had come from a monkey, I was going to die and rot, and until then, I was supposed to live my life like an animal. Then the school counselor had the nerve to ask me why I was always depressed! Hearing this would depress any rational person.

When people are told they are animals, why are we surprised that crime is out of control, teenagers are having babies, and people are becoming more and more brutal toward one another?

The point of this book was to help you to de-program from some of the world's propaganda and replace it with a Christlike way of thinking and acting. We are spiritual beings, created in God's image. We are on our way to live in his kingdom forever, but until then, we are here to glorify Jesus with every tiny decision we make.

Jesus has given us all the tools we need to make those choices just as he would. We have his Spirit, and we have the pages of the New Testament which give us his own wonderful "example." Now it is up to you and me to remember at every one of life's little crossroads to pause briefly and ask, "If it were him and not me facing this, what would Jesus do?"

We want to hear from you. Please send your comments about this book to us in care of the address below. Thank you.

ZondervanPublishingHouse
Grand Rapids, Michigan 49530
http://www.zondervan.com

Dana Key may be contacted at
dkey7@aol.com